G. B. Shaw
«Pygmalion»

Contents

The Author and His Times

Pygmalion is one of George Bernard Shaw's most popular plays. He wrote it in 1912, but it was not performed in London until 1914. Before that it was shown to audiences all over the world and was a huge success everywhere. In 1956 the musical adaptation of it, *My Fair Lady*, was first performed in New York and became one of the most successful musicals ever.

George Bernard Shaw was born in Dublin in 1856. In his long life of ninety-four years he wrote over fifty dramas and countless essays and political pamphlets.

At the time Ireland was ruled by Protestant England and since the Shaws were Protestants, they were associated with the wealthy, pro-English élite. Like the rest of the Protestant minority, Shaw's family felt they were superior to the Catholics. At school, for instance, Bernard was not allowed to associate with his Catholic schoolmates. But in reality the family had very little money and led a disorganised life. Mr Shaw, an Englishman, was a grain merchant. He could not run his business and drank heavily. His Irish wife tried to keep up a respectable facade. She loved music and preferred it to housework or looking after the children, so they were rather neglected. Through his mother Bernard learned to love music and the knowledge he gained enabled him to work as a music critic later on. When Mrs Shaw could no longer stand her domestic life she moved to London to teach singing. Bernard's formal education was poor and constantly interrupted. But he had a thirst for knowledge and read widely.

At fifteen Bernard left school and went to work in a

Dublin office. Five years later he decided to become a novelist and joined his mother in London. For nine years he took on various odd jobs, but was financially dependent on his mother. During this time he continued educating himself.

Bernard soon began to attend debating societies, where a frequent topic was the state of society, particularly that of the working classes. In those days the upper and upper middle classes were wealthy and powerful, but the working classes led miserable lives in the factories and slums. Shaw became involved in these issues and soon became a popular public speaker. In 1884, aged twenty-eight, he joined the new Fabian Society.

The Fabians wanted to bring about economic and social reforms in England by getting new laws passed. Besides speaking in public, Shaw also wrote many leaflets, newspaper and magazine articles for them. By the end of Shaw's life, in the 1950s, the Welfare State had been established, women had won the right to vote and free education was avaliable to everyone from five to fifteen. Many of these improvements were the result of the changed climate of opinion which the Fabians – and also Shaw's plays – helped to create. All his life G.B.S., as he was known, drew attention to the evils caused by poverty. *Pygmalion*, for example, shows the discrepancy between the deprivation and insecurity of the poor and the comfort and even luxury of the upper and upper middle classes.

Shaw's career as a writer started in 1885 at the age of twenty-nine, when he began to review books, art and music. He amused and shocked the public with his original and witty comments. He attacked the fashionable, artificial plays of the time and praised dramas which discussed ideas and social problems, such as those of the revolutionary new Norwegian playwright

Henrik Ibsen (1828-1906). Shaw's criticism played an important part in the revival of drama in England.

G.B.S. was a striking figure, tall and thin with a bright red beard. He was a militant vegetarian, teetotaller and non-smoker. He held very strong opinions on almost everything and always said exactly what he thought, so that most of his life he was surrounded by controversy. In 1898 he married a wealthy upper class Irishwoman and fellow Fabian Socialist, Charlotte Payne Townshend. From then on he no longer needed to work as a journalist and could devote himself to writing dramas. However, he did not become really famous until he was over forty. Between 1892 and 1940 he wrote about 50 plays, the first when he was 36 and the last at the age of 93. He was the most popular playwright in Europe and was awarded the Nobel prize in 1926. When he died in 1950, aged ninety-four, he was a millionaire.

Shaw was not primarily interested in the theatre, but in politics. He only started to write plays when he realised that this was the best way to publicise his socialist views. In fact, he added prefaces to his dramas to make sure that people really understood his ideas. The theme of *Pygmalion*, for example, is explained in the preface. Shaw realised that in his society the way people spoke determined their position in society: 'it is impossible for an Englishman to open his mouth without making some other Englishman despise him'.

When he entered the English theatre it was very mediocre. For over a century the plays had been of a very poor quality. The theatre had completely lost touch with the real world. The topics, language, acting and scenery were all highly improbable and 'theatrical'. It was not thought important to create realistic characters and situations, and true feelings were replaced by cliché and sentimentality. Audiences wanted plays to entertain them and to provide a romanticised substitute for real life. One of the most popular types of plays was melodrama with its clear-cut, black and white patterns of good and evil. Theatre-goers expected to see their own stereotyped ideas confirmed on stage.

Shaw's great contribution was to free the theatre from the Victorian ideals of the time by presenting his audiences with unconventional ways of seeing things. He established a completely new type of play, of acting and of stage production. It was not only his more realistic style which was new, but also what he had to say, for it was revolutionary to deal with social, political, philosophical and religious issues on stage. All his dramas have some sort of message. Yet the significant thing about Shavian drama was not so much the kind of topics he introduced, but the fact that he brought ideas into the theatre at all. Shaw's revolutionary new genre has been described as the *play of ideas*, the *problem* or *discussion play*, the *comedy of ideas* or the *corrective comedy*. He did not try to tell his audience what to think, but only asked them to be realistic and at least search for the truth, instead of simply repeating comfortable, conventional ideas. He was more interested in creating understanding and sensitivity towards social problems than in detailed solutions. For him the theatre was a means of making his audience rethink their out-dated beliefs and of improving social conditions. His concern with social justice runs through all his works.

Most of Shaw's forty-odd plays, mainly comedies, challenged the established order. He exposed the snobbery and hypocrisy of his society and ridiculed many of its conventional norms and values, for instance about love, marriage, morality, democracy, religion and people's blind faith in science. In his opinion politicians, scientists, theologians and the powerful middle classes were imprisoned by formulas, habit and complacency. But his main quarrel with society was its injustice. He was deeply disillusioned with a government whose main concern was to protect private property and expand the British Empire. In addition, he was extremely hostile to capitalism, which he blamed for most economic, social and moral ills. By ridiculing capitalism as inefficient, unjust and out-of-date Shaw played a decisive part in changing the whole atmosphere of political thinking. It was largely due to his influence that large numbers of the middle classes and the intelligentsia accepted the Labour Party, which began to form at the end of the nineteenth century.

Yet Shaw was not only a destructive critic. He postulated a kind of faith which he called the "Creative Evolution". According to him, everyone has in them a "Life Force", and he believed that if people searched for self-awareness and self-knowledge this Life Force would make the world a peaceful, happy place. By stimulating thought and self-criticism in his audiences he tried to make them develop a greater awareness of themselves and of the world around them.

The weapons which Shaw used to strip away illusion and make people look at life more realistically were humour, paradox and irony. His method was to take familiar ideas and situations and to present them in new, surprising ways in order to make his audience see things differently. For instance, where they expected tragedy he gave them comedy and after climaxes he brought them down to earth, making them realise that life goes on and that the problems had not been magically solved. When the audience saw the title *Pygmalion*, for example, they would expect a love story, like the Greek legend from which the play takes its name. This expectation would be reinforced if they read the play, because Shaw gave it the sub-title, 'A Romance'. Watching it, they would be reminded of the Cinderella fairy story and would expect a happy, romantic ending. By subtly changing things into their opposites Shaw destroyed illusions. This element of paradox paved the way for modern drama, in which orthodox ideas are often questioned and audiences are shocked out of complacency by being brought face to face with reality.

At first Shaw could not find anyone willing to stage his plays in London. Theatre managers refused his work because it did not contain the predictable actions and sentimental scenes they expected. Audiences were horrified and confused and critics complained that he used the stage as a lecture platform. So he had no alternative but to have his plays produced abroad. Gradually, however, although London audiences continued to be shocked, they began to enjoy his dramas and were even willing to listen to his arguments if they were also amusing. Eventually they got used to seeing serious subjects discussed on stage and to a more naturalistic style of acting and setting.

Shaw lived through two World Wars and his whole lifetime covered a period of tremendous social change. In the nineteenth century Britain found itself in a conflict between traditional concepts of an eternal, God-given order and the new science, with its evolutionary interpretations of the world. The great challenge to Shaw's society were the new developments in industry and technology. It is against this background that we must see Shaw's constant warnings that society needs to free itself of conventional ways of thinking and react to changes with an open mind if it is to progress. In his dramas he tried to assert and strengthen free will and imagination, which he saw as an important means of adapting to new situations. He told his audiences that man is capable of shaping his own destiny.

Shaw's distrust of oversimplification and his ability to live with uncertainty and ambiguity reflected his whole way of seeing the world. He found life so complex that nothing was black and white. He would not accept easy answers just because they provided a sense of security. He always saw many different sides to a question and these were often contradictory. So to him paradox was the essence of life. He hated the complacency of those who believed they had found the Truth. To Shaw's mind the only certainty was that everything was always uncertain and in a state of constant change.

SOME OF SHAW'S MOST IMPORTANT PLAYS
(in order of publication)

Mrs Warren's Profession	1898
Arms and the Man	1898
Candida	1898
Man and Superman	1903
Major Barbara	1907
Androcles and the Lion	1916
Pygmalion	1916
Saint Joan	1924

The Plot ✓

Pygmalion is the story of a young woman who is transformed into a duchess. The girl, Eliza Doolittle, is selling flowers in Covent Garden market when she is overheard by Professor Higgins, a teacher of phonetics. He remarks that her Cockney accent will keep her in the gutter for the rest of her life and boasts that in six months time he could remove all traces of Liza's Cockney accent and could even pass her off as a duchess at a high society party. His friend, Colonel Pickering, bets that he will not be able to do it.

Higgins' housekeeper, Mrs Pearce, accuses the two men of behaving irresponsibly. They are planning to amuse themselves without thinking of the consequences for Eliza when their experiment is finished. But they ignore her and Eliza goes to live with Higgins and Pickering for the next six months. Eliza's father, Alfred Doolittle, has never shown much interest in his daughter, but he now calls on Higgins and demands compensation. Eventually he offers to sell her for five pounds.

Eliza is a quick, intelligent pupil and after three months Higgins decides that it is time for her first test, so he takes her to his mother's at-home afternoon. By chance, the other guests are the same people who were sheltering from the rain at the beginning of the play, the Eynsford Hills. The son, Freddy, immediately falls in love with Eliza and the daughter, Clara, is also very impressed by her. Nevertheless, Eliza fails her test because her conversation sounds very unnatural. Higgins realises that it is not enough to teach her how to pronounce her words correctly, but that he must also educate her mind. Like Mrs Pearce, his mother tries to warn him of the consequences of the experiment for Eliza, but he ignores her.

Six months later Higgins wins his bet: Eliza is taken for a princess at a high society garden party. However, after the experiment Higgins takes all the credit for himself. Both he and Pickering completely neglect her, and do not even bother to thank her. Eliza realises that they only saw her as an interesting experiment and that now it is over she will be dropped. She suddenly realises the position she is in. She cannot go back to her old life, but she does not fit in with her new surroundings either. She has no means of earning a living and must rely on finding a rich husband. First she is desperately unhappy, then angry because Higgins has behaved irresponsibly towards her. They quarrel and she throws his slipper at him.

The next morning Eliza has gone. Higgins goes out looking for her and calls at his mother's. He is surprised to find Eliza there. Before he can see her they are interrupted by the arrival of Doolittle, now transformed into a gentleman. As a joke Higgins once recommended him as a public speaker to an American millionaire and when the millionaire died he left Alfred an income of three thousand pounds a year. As a result, the former vulgar dustman has become respectable. But, paradoxically, he is now thoroughly miserable.

Higgins tries to bully Eliza into returning home with him. But he has not noticed that during the past few months she has changed. She will no longer let him be rude to her and treat her as a servant. She wants to be treated as an equal. But Higgins is incapable of this. He cannot change his behaviour. He only seems to want her back because she acts as his secretary and he cannot manage without her, not because of any real affection for her.

Under these conditions Eliza refuses to return and

considers the alternative of marrying Freddy. Eliza and Mrs Higgins go off to Doolittle's wedding and Higgins stays behind, obviously expecting Eliza to go back home with him and that everything will be as before. The question of what is to become of Eliza is left open. Nevertheless, we are left feeling optimistic. Eliza has become more self-confident and is now more in control of her life. Her actual alternatives do not seem so important. However, in those days audiences, actors and theatre critics were not used to open endings. They wanted to know exactly what happened. It was probably because Shaw felt pressurised to explain that he wrote a sequel informing us that Eliza married Freddy and opened a flower shop.

Act One

Higgins notes down everything Liza says in phonetics. He tells Pickering that he teaches people to improve their accents so that they can move in higher circles. He boasts that after six months with him people would take Eliza for a duchess.

Act Two

Liza calls on Higgins to ask for lessons. Pickering bets him that he will not be able to pass her off as a duchess at an ambassador's garden party in six months time. Higgins accepts and Liza comes to live with them. Doolittle sells Liza to Higgins.

Act Three

Liza fails her first test at Mrs Higgins's 'at-home' day. Mrs Higgins warns her son and Pickering that they are behaving irresponsibly.

Act Four

Higgins, Pickering and Eliza have returned from the Embassy reception, where she won Higgins's bet for him. But both men ignore her. Eliza sees that she has been used. After quarrelling with Higgins she leaves. Outside, Freddy is waiting for her.

Act Five

Higgins and Pickering go to Henry's mother's to tell her about Eliza's disappearance. She is furious with them. Doolittle arrives, dressed as a gentleman. Eliza enters, now a perfect lady. She refuses to go back with Higgins on his terms.

Summary of the Play ✓

THE PREFACE

Shaw wrote plays in order to explain his socialist ideas to people. To make sure they were understood properly he gave them prefaces. Also, his plays were so controversial that at first no one was willing to stage them, so he had them published as books instead and additional prefaces gave the public better value for money. The books were actually read as much for the prefaces as for the plays.

The preface to *Pygmalion* states the main theme of the play, that in Shaw's society there was a strong link between the way people spoke and their social position, 'it is impossible for an Englishman to open his mouth without making some other Englishman despise him'. As a socialist Shaw fought against inequality and used *Pygmalion* to attack class divisions and the snobbish attitudes of the upper and upper middle classes towards the less privileged. Through his play he implied that getting rid of 'low' accents would help to make society more equal. At the end of the preface he encourages people with 'accents that cut them off from all high employment' to try to improve their chances in life by changing their accent: 'the change wrought by Professor Higgins is neither impossible nor uncommon. The modern concierge's daughter who fulfils her ambition by playing the Queen of Spain in Ruy Blas at the Théatre Francais is only one of many thousands of men and women who have sloughed off their native dialects and acquired a new tongue'.

The preface also explains Shaw's dislike of the English spelling system. He felt it was too complicated because from reading the words it was impossible to tell what they sounded like. In the words *tough*, *bough*, *cough* and *dough*, for instance, the letter sequence *ough* is spelt the same, but pronounced differently in each case. He wanted to replace the traditional spelling system by a phonetic one, so that the words would be written exactly as they were spoken. He felt so strongly about this that he wrote about it in *Pygmalion*: 'The reformer we need most today is an energetic phonetic enthusiast: that is why I have made such a one the hero of a popular play' (preface). One way to simplify English spelling, suggested Shaw, would be to use the American *-or* and *-ize* instead of the British *-our*, as in *honour* and *-ise* (*realise*). He also simplified the use of apostrophes and left them out in some words where there could be no misunderstanding, for instance *dont*, *havent*, or *Ive*.

At the end of the preface Shaw explains that he is deliberately using *Pygmalion* to teach his audience something, as indeed he always did. He boasts that its success proves that a didactic play is not necessarily boring. He actually believed that art could never be important unless it dealt with some aspect of contemporary life. *Pygmalion*, he said, 'is so intensely and deliberately didactic, and its subject is esteemed so dry, that I delight in throwing it at the heads of the wiseacres who repeat the parrot cry that art should never be didactic. It goes to prove my contention that great art can never be anything else'.

ACT ONE

The play is set in London at the beginning of the twentieth century. It begins late at night in Covent Garden vegetable market. People are running for shelter from the rain and whistles are blowing everywhere for taxis. A group is standing in the entrance to St Paul's

Church. Among them is a lady and her daughter in evening dress, who have probably just been to the theatre. They are later introduced as Mrs Eynsford Hill and Clara. The lady's son, Freddy, has gone to find a taxi. When he returns without one they send him off again. As he runs off he bumps into a flower seller (Liza Doolittle), knocking her basket of flowers out of her hands. She calls after him, by chance using his correct name. His mother wants to know how such a girl can know her son and starts talking to her. Eventually she compensates her for the flowers.

The group is then joined by an elderly, military-looking man (Colonel Pickering), also in evening dress. When the girl tries to sell him a flower he refuses, but still gives her some small change. She is warned against taking the money by a bystander, who tells her that there is a man writing down everything she says. Liza is afraid that she will be reported to the police and accused of addressing men for immoral purposes. She becomes hysterical and protests her innocence. The note taker denies any connection with the police. He shows Liza what he has written, but she cannot read it because it is written with the symbols of the phonetic alphabet. He reads her words out in a perfect imitation of her Cockney accent and then amazes the bystanders by telling them exactly where they come from by their speech. In the meantime it has stopped raining. Everyone leaves except the note-taker, the gentleman and the flower girl.

By this time all the main characters have been introduced. Shaw chose a setting which would enable him to bring together people from very different backgrounds. The use of general terms to describe them – 'THE MOTHER, THE FLOWER GIRL, THE BYSTANDER' – suggests that the author wanted to widen the reference of his play and encourage his audience to think of types of people rather than individuals. He presents us with representatives of the different classes of people living in London at the time, ranging from the aristocratic Eynsford Hills, who are used to going to the theatre and riding around in taxis, to the poverty-stricken flower girl.

Gradually the mood calms down as Liza is reassured that she will not be reported to the police, and Pickering starts talking to Higgins. This change of tone is underlined by a change in the weather, for the storm passes and the rain stops.

We learn that the note taker is Henry Higgins, an expert on phonetics, and the gentleman, Colonel Pickering, is an authority on Indian dialects. They know each other's work and have been wanting to meet. Higgins tells his new friend that he makes a living from teaching people from humble backgrounds to speak with an upper class accent so that they can move in higher social circles. He uses Liza as an example, saying that because of her accent she is condemned to a life of poverty. He boasts that in six months he could give her an upper class accent and pass her off as a duchess at, for instance, an ambassador's garden party.

As the two men go off together Eliza tries to sell them some flowers to pay for her rent. Hearing the church bells, Higgins is reminded that he should be charitable and throws her a handful of coins. To Liza this is a fortune and she is overjoyed. Freddy returns with a taxi, but finds that his mother and sister have gone home. Taxis represent wealth and prestige to Liza so she decides to spend some of her money on the luxury of riding home in one. Since she does not want Freddy to know what a poor area she lives in she orders the driver to take her to Buckingham Palace. But her home is a miserable, cold, damp room in a slum. One of Shaw's main intentions when writing *Pygmalion* was to draw attention to the terrible conditions in which the working class were living. This description of Liza's room points an accusing finger at the gulf between the lives of the working class and those of the more privileged members of society.

During the first Act we get a general impression of the main characters. Shaw helps us to form these impressions by his extremely detailed stage directions.

Higgins is an expert in his field, but seems cold and unfeeling. He cannot understand Liza's distress and shouts at her instead of trying to console her. Pickering is the one who tries to reassure her. Higgins is very rude, talking about Liza as if she were not there and calling her a 'squashed cabbage'. He only expresses any sensitivity when he talks about the English language, which he loves. To him it is the language of beautiful literature and the means by which man expresses his soul. It really seems to pain him when people do not speak it well.

Colonel Pickering is the complete opposite of Higgins – amiable, kindly, understanding and generous. Before he gets to know Liza he shows sympathy for her by giving her some coins without buying a flower.

Liza, despite her poverty, is cheerful and lively. When Freddy spoils her flowers she has the self-confidence to demand compensation from her betters. From her protestations of innocence we learn that she is emotional and that she has great self-respect. Her defiant gesture of riding home in a taxi suggests that she has imagination and ambition and would like to rise in society if she could. This is also implied by the pictures of fashionable dresses on her wall.

The contrast with Clara Eynsford Hill could not be greater. She is apparently used to a life of luxury and has no sympathy at all for the likes of Liza. She even tries to persuade her mother not to compensate her for the flowers. Clara is haughty, bad-tempered, selfish, bossy and impatient. Her mother seems much more pleasant. Her brother, Freddy, seems to be weak and rather lacking in initiative. He fails to get a taxi (in contrast to Higgins) and allows his mother and daughter to bully him.

By the end of the first Act, then, the main characters have been introduced and the audience knows what the play is going to be about. The action proceeds rapidly and the audience's interest is sustained by a variety of characters and changes of mood: the first group of people we meet are the Eynsford Hills, then there is the incident with Freddy, followed by various conversations involving different groups of people – Liza, Mrs Eynsford Hill and Clara; Pickering and Liza; Liza, the bystander and Higgins and so on.

ACT TWO

Act two takes place in Higgins's laboratory, which is also his living room. He has just finished demonstrating his equipment and methods to Pickering when his housekeeper, Mrs Pearce, announces with some surprise that a young woman wants to speak to him. He is puzzled, but agrees to see her because he thinks she might be useful for his work. The girl is Liza, looking tidier and cleaner than usual. Higgins is disappointed and rudely tells her to leave. But Liza insists. She does not realise that the night before, when Higgins had talked about improving her accent and getting her a job in a shop, he had only been using her as an example. Liza, however, took him seriously and now she has come for lessons.

Pickering reminds Higgins of his boast that in six months – three if she learns quickly – he could pass Liza off as a duchess. He bets all the expenses of the experiment that his friend will not succeed. Higgins accepts the challenge and tells Mrs Pearce to clean her up and get her some new clothes. This frightens Liza because she does not understand his intentions. Also, apart from his rudeness, she has never heard anyone speak like Higgins before and concludes that he must be mad. She does not realise that he loves to play with words. Eventually Higgins resorts to alternately bullying her and tempting her with the kind of life she will be able to lead if she agrees.

Yet despite Higgins's bullying, rudeness, and thoughtlessness he remains a likeable figure because of his tremendous energy, his love of his work and his wit. He is not mean or small-minded, but rather like a spoilt child who cannot keep his emotions under control. Pickering forms a sharp contrast to him. Whereas Higgins's violence frightens Liza, Pickering's calmness and politeness soothes and reassures her. Both Mrs Pearce and the Colonel are shocked by the professor's rudeness and insensitivity. The housekeeper warns that the experiment is irresponsible and asks Higgins to consider the possible consequences for the girl. However, he is so fascinated by the task ahead of him that he overrides all objections. It is clear that Higgins does not think of her as a human being with feelings, but rather as an inanimate object or a doll for him to experiment with. He is like a small boy with a new toy.

Liza herself is confused. She is not sure how to react to Higgins, but is reassured by the Colonel's behaviour. For the first time in her life she is treated with courtesy and addressed as 'Miss Doolittle'. This gives her a sense of her own value as a person. She is also tempted by the promise of chocolates and taxi rides. But, more importantly, she really would like to sell flowers in a shop instead of on the streets.

Finally Mrs Pearce takes Liza off to the bathroom. The scene is highly amusing and illustrates Shaw's

talent as a playwright. For after the conflict and tension
of the previous scene it provides welcome comic relief.
But, as always in Shavian drama, the comedy has a
serious side to it. Shaw shows his audience that people
who have to live like Liza do not have adequate sanitation or heating. Liza has never had a bath in her life
and does not even know what a bathtub is. From the
description of her room we know that she has no hot
water and very little heat. She has never slept in a warm
bed and could not afford nightwear even if she knew
that it existed. She tells Mrs Pearce how she dreads
being cold. Shaw makes sure that the audience does
not miss the point as Liza tells her father how easy it is
to keep clean if hot water, towels and soap are so easily
available: 'Now I know why ladies is so clean. Washing's
a treat for them. Wish they could see what it is for the
like of me!'.

After a while Mrs Pearce returns and asks Higgins to
be more careful about his manners when Liza is around
so that he will set her a good example. The conversation
is very amusing and reveals the discrepancy between
Higgins's image of himself and reality. He never reflects
about himself and is so arrogant that he cannot believe
he ever does anything wrong. Nevertheless, he is so entertaining that we forgive him and perhaps no longer
take him seriously.

The arrival of Alfred Doolittle provides a new focus of
interest. It also illustrates Shaw's dramatic technique of
regularly introducing new characters as a play progresses in order to prevent the audience from becoming
bored. Alfred's arrival introduces an element of suspense when we are told that he is Liza's father. He has
come to protest against the abduction of his daughter,
suggesting that Higgins has taken her for immoral purposes. But Higgins disarms him by immediately agree-
ing to give Liza back. Doolittle is forced to abandon his

role of the outraged father and offers to sell her for five pounds. Higgins is impressed by Alfred's natural eloquence and highly amused by his unconventional opinions. For Alfred represents the very opposite of contemporary moral standards. He is a rogue who openly admits that all he wants is to get as much pleasure as possible out of life. He has no sense of responsibility whatsoever and only shows interest in Liza when he thinks he can make money out of her. Yet, as with Higgins, he is likeable because of his complete honesty. He does not even pretend to have a conscience. He is also very original and amusing. Because he is so entertaining it does not seem to matter that he is hardly a realistic dustman and that his speech on middle class morality sounds rather forced.

Eventually Higgins agrees to the sale of Liza, despite pangs of conscience. As Alfred is leaving he bumps into his daughter, now washed and dressed in a kimono. She already looks so different that he does not recognise her at first. When he has gone she says she never wants to see him again, which is understandable in view of the beatings he used to give her. Already there are signs of a growing self-awareness in her. She would like to take a taxi to Tottenham Court Road to show off to the other girls. Higgins, however, warns her against snobbery. Her delight when Mrs Pearce announces the arrival of her new clothes is a signal that she is beginning to enjoy her new life.

By the end of Act two the exposition is complete: the main characters have been introduced, we know what the story will be about and hints have been given as to how the characters will develop. Liza's transformation has begun.

There follows a short scene, which Shaw marked as optional, showing what Liza's lessons were like. Higgins is so restless and impatient that he makes her cry, although he is pleased with her. Without the Colonel's support and encouragement she would probably have given up before long. But she learns quickly and we can see that she might be able to win the bet, that is, if she can stand Higgins long enough.

ACT THREE

A few months later Higgins decides to give Liza her first test at his mother's 'at-home day'. But when he bursts in on Mrs Higgins, unannounced, she asks him to leave because his bad manners always offend her friends. This meeting is a comic reversal of the usual pattern of a mother being glad to see her son. He tells her about Liza and explains that she will be calling in later.

The introduction of a new character, Mrs Higgins, again shows how Shaw tries to keep the audience's interest alive. Her room is described in great detail. In contrast to her son's living room, hers is spacious and uncluttered. The furnishings are elegant and in good taste. The room and Mrs Higgins herself embody the gracious style of living enjoyed by the upper middle class.

Mrs Higgins's first visitors are Mrs Eynsford Hill and her daughter Clara, who were sheltering from the rain in the first Act. Higgins does not recognise them yet. They are followed by Pickering and Freddy. While he is waiting for Liza Higgins is very rude, making it obvious that he is impatient for the others to leave again. He clearly finds small talk a complete waste of time. His mother constantly rebukes him. He then remembers hearing Clara's and Freddy's voices somewhere before, but does not remember where.

Finally Liza arrives, looking very beautiful. Freddy immediately falls in love with her. Suddenly Higgins re-

members where he first met the Eynsford Hills and
fears that everything might be spoilt. But no one recognises the former flower girl. Liza makes a great impression. She not only looks beautiful, but also moves very
gracefully. She talks, as instructed, only about the
weather and people's health. It is obvious that every
sentence has been carefully rehearsed. The problem is
not *how* she speaks, but *what* she says. She uses far
too formal a register for such a social occasion and this
makes her speech sound mechanical, like a robot's. But
gradually she begins to feel more at ease, which is
where the trouble starts. As she relaxes she becomes
more spontaneous and speaks of topics which were
taboo at such gatherings. She also forgets her grammar.
The contrast between her elegant appearance, cultured
pronunciation and vulgar speech is extremely comical.
Higgins tries to save the situation by explaining that she
is using the latest small talk. Everyone accepts this, but
the swear word she uses when leaving creates a sensa-
tion. At the time the word *bloody* also scandalised London theatre-goers since such vulgar expressions were
not normally used on stage. Mrs Eynsford Hill is
shocked, but the impressionable Clara feels that her
mother is being old-fashioned and even imitates Liza in
order to prove how modern she is. Here Shaw is ridiculing the snobbishness and pretentiousness of high
society. For Clara, who refused to have anything to do
with Liza the flower girl, now admires Miss Doolittle so
much that she takes her as a model. Shaw might also
be suggesting that the social élite is easily taken in by
illusion and even prefers it to reality.

Despite her blunder, Higgins and Pickering are
pleased with Eliza's performance. But Mrs Higgins dis-
illusions them. She accuses both her son and Pickering
of acting like babies, amusing themselves with a toy.
Like Mrs Pearce, she tries to make them realise that

they are behaving irresponsibly. But they do not understand her and protest that they do nothing else but
think of Eliza. They also praise Eliza's quick ear. Apparently she is exceptionally good at imitating sounds,
even better than Higgins himself. She has learned to
play the piano and can, for example, play everything she
hears by ear. However, the question of Eliza's future
does not interest them. She seems to be nothing more
than the subject of an interesting experiment. They do
not see that after the experiment she will no longer belong in her old environment but will not be fit for any
other kind of life either.

Higgins rejects his mother's accusations, boasting
that he has given Eliza so many advantages that she will
be able to find her own way in the world. His mother
scoffs at this and warns that Eliza might find herself in
a similar position to that of Mrs Eynsford Hill. Although
the Eynsford Hills no longer have enough money to
keep up their social position, they are prevented from
going out to earn a living because of their social status.
As Mrs Higgins puts it, her friend has 'the manners and
habits that disqualify a fine lady from earning her own
living without giving her a fine lady's income!'. Through
this comment Shaw is attacking the rigid social conventions which dominated the lives of the upper and
middle classes. He implies that it would be better if
people like the Eynsford Hills could accept their position honestly and try to do something about it instead
of trying to preserve an appearance of respectability.

Higgins and Pickering leave, laughing as they anti-
cipate the fun they will get from their next experiment
with Eliza. It is interesting that as the flower girl
changes into a lady the name by which she used to be
known, Liza, is replaced by the more formal Eliza. So
far, Pygmalion has only half succeeded in bringing his
Galatea to life (see Themes, 4). But there are definite

signs that Eliza's hidden beauty and talents are gradually emerging.

The Embassy reception

Originally Shaw did not include this scene in the play. He added it later when it was pointed out to him that he had 'omitted' it. This shows that he himself did not regard it as so important. Being more interested in psychological processes than actions, he probably felt that the climax was rather the conflict between Eliza and Higgins in Act 4.

At the reception Eliza's beauty and elegance are admired by all. There is a moment of suspense when one of Higgins's former pupils appears, a Hungarian called Nepommuck. Higgins is afraid that he will expose Eliza as a fraud. However, his elementary grammar mistakes make us wonder if he is really as much of an expert as he pretends. Eliza is safe. Nepommuck pronounces that she is not English at all, but a Hungarian princess. Again we see Shaw's love of irony as he pokes fun at Nepommuck's arrogance and exposes his incompetence.

The scene is another illustration of Higgins's impatience with formal social occasions and his refusal to make any concessions. Not only is he rude to everyone, but he also neglects Eliza. It is Pickering who helps her to get over her nerves, helping her out of the car, showing her the ladies' room and generally reassuring her. Up to this point we have traced Eliza's external development, the changes in her appearance, speech and manners. Mrs Higgins's 'at-home' was the half-way mark. From now on she develops in a more spiritual way as she develops her mind and soul.

ACT FOUR

It is midnight in Higgins' laboratory. The professor, Pickering and Eliza have just returned from the ambassador's reception, a dinner and the opera. Eliza, in evening dress, has passed her test brilliantly, but is now very tired. She sits and listens as the two men discuss the evening. Higgins is relieved that the whole thing is over. He takes all the credit for himself and even Pickering regards Eliza's success as a reflection of his friend's skill. Then Higgins says that during the last few months he found the experiment dreadfully boring. Both men completely ignore Eliza and talk about her as if she were not in the room.

Eliza is disappointed. She has done her best, but has not received a single word of praise or thanks. Her disappointment turns to anger when she notices that she has been used as a guinea-pig and that her teachers no longer need her. This is a shock. Now she suddenly realises that she is back where she started – even worse, for she cannot go back to her old life.

As the two men go to bed Higgins gives Eliza his orders for the next day, just as if she were his servant. In anger and despair Eliza throws herself on the floor. Then Higgins comes back for his slippers and she hurls them at him. He is astonished and demands an explanation. When she explains he still does not takes her seriously. This is where his complete lack of understanding and sympathy for other people becomes most obvious. He suggests that they might be able to find someone willing to marry her, not realising how offensive this is. In a typical Shavian paradox Shaw suggests that it is more degrading for a woman to offer herself on the marriage market than to go out to work for a living. Here again he is criticising the bourgeois moral code which ruled that it was degrading for a woman of any social standing to earn her own living. Instead she was expected to provide for herself through marriage. The scene is given a deeper meaning considering that the suffragette movement was just beginning in England. Shaw himself always gave it his strong support. He insisted that 'family life will never be decent ... until this central horror of the dependence of women on men is done away with.' (Solomon 1962, p. 356)

What, then, is to become of Eliza? In her former life she was capable of earning her own living, but as a 'lady' this is denied her. It seems as if her only alternative is really to find a husband. The audience is forced to wonder whether the experiment was really such a good idea.

Suddenly Eliza changes her tone and addresses Higgins as 'sir'. This amazes him because it implies that she is his servant. Then she asks whether her new clothes belong to her because she does not want to be accused of stealing them if she takes them away with her. This angers and hurts Higgins. Eliza knows very well that he is not mean or petty and would never even think of asking her to give anything back. Eliza has her revenge. She knows that he prides himself on always being in control of himself and plays on this weak spot by goading him into a display of anger. Also, he has hurt her feelings so often that now she demonstrates that she can hurt him, too. But still he does not understand. Both leave the room in a rage.

The following optional scene describes how Eliza changes into her outdoor clothes and leaves the house. Outside she meets Freddy, who admits that he spends most nights outside the house, hoping to catch a glimpse of her. Lonely and despairing, Eliza responds to his declaration of love. In those days policemen did not tolerate couples kissing in public, so they are forced to ride round in a taxi all night. We learn in Act 5 that the next morning they went to ask advice from Mrs Hggins.

Freddy is the complete opposite of Higgins. He is patient, gentle, and absolutely devoted to Eliza. It is not surprising that after Higgins's constant criticism she finds it rather pleasant to be worshipped by someone. Higgins only paid attention to her as a pupil, but completely ignored her as a human being.

Act 4 marks a turning point in the relationship between Liza and her teacher. Whereas up to now Higgins was rather contemptuous of Liza, now it is she who is beginning to despise him. Pygmalion's statue has finally come alive, but Shaw gives the legend a typical ironic twist. Unlike Galatea, Eliza is no longer willing to be treated as someone else's creation and rebels against her teacher.

Besides the *Pygmalion* legend, the audience would also be reminded of the *Cinderella* fairy tale, in which a poor, downtrodden girl is transformed into a princess, goes to a ball and finally marries the prince she meets there. But with Shaw they wait in vain for a happy ending. He always tried to prove to his audiences that illusions are worthless and that it is far better to look at life realistically. So Eliza does not become Galatea, nor does she marry her prince and live happily ever after. With Shaw the climax does not automatically solve problems. They are still there the next day.

ACT FIVE

The following day Higgins and Pickering call on Henry's mother to inform her that Liza has disappeared. When she hears that they have informed the police she is very annoyed, accusing them of behaving as if they owned the girl. She does not tell them that Eliza is upstairs and gives instructions for Eliza not to come down until she is sent for. Her son seems more upset by the inconvenience which Eliza's absence is causing him than by any real concern for her. She has been arranging his appointments and looking after his possessions.

This conversation is interrupted by the arrival of Doolittle. He enters, beautifully dressed and apparently wealthy. Surprisingly, he has not come about his daughter, but to accuse Higgins of destroying his happiness. As a result of a casual remark in a letter which Higgins wrote to an American millionaire, Doolittle has been left an annual income of three thousand pounds, on condition that he gives lectures in support of moral reform. This means that he now belongs to the middle class and is forced to support the moral standards which as a dustman he rejected. Not only that, he now finds that all sorts of people keep trying to sell him services and laying claims to him. Doctors insist on constantly checking his health, he has to pay servants to do things he previously had no need for and suddenly lots of newfound relatives are asking him for money. Since he cannot resist the temptation of the inheritance he feels trapped. Here again we see how Shaw uses paradox to turn accepted codes and values upside down.

With the appearance of Eliza's father Mrs Higgins sees a new possibility of solving the girl's problems, thinking that Doolittle will now support her. However, Higgins protests that Eliza belongs to him, not to her father, since he bought her for five pounds. His jealousy has nothing to do with any personal feelings for Eliza, but rather shows that he sees her as his property and does not want to lose his masterpiece.

Doolittle's arrival adds variety to the action as the conflict between Eliza and Higgins is temporarily overshadowed. But, typically with Shaw, there is a serious side to the dustman's story. His rise could be seen as a warning that a higher social status does not necessarily bring happiness. Although Doolittle is unhappy in his new position, he does not have the strength of character to resist its temptations. Shaw often uses such parallels and contrasts to make a point. Both Eliza and her father move up in society and in each case this is reflected in their outer appearance. But whereas Doolittle has been turned into a gentleman by external forces, the change in Eliza's position was due to her own efforts. The contrast between what happens to Eliza and her father expresses Shaw's belief that people are able to improve their lives through their own efforts, but that they must retain their integrity. Alfred is a warning that people should not allow themselves to become slaves to the standards and conventions of others, but should develop their own personal, flexible code of behaviour.

The conflict between Eliza and Higgins is then taken up again as Henry's mother reveals that Eliza is upstairs. She explains that the girl was angry and frightened and reproaches her son for his behaviour the previous night. He is incapable of seeing that he might have been at fault, but gradually Pickering begins to understand and is ashamed. Mrs Higgins agrees to ask Eliza to come down on condition that Henry is polite to her. Tactfully, she asks Doolittle to go out onto the balcony so that the shock to his daughter will not be so great.

Eliza enters, calm and dignified, the perfect lady. In contrast to her father, she has regained her old self-confidence, whereas he has lost his. She does not allow Higgins to upset her and ignores his attempts to treat her as his property. She addresses Higgins and Pickering formally, as if they were no more than slight acquaintances. This enrages Higgins because it is he who taught her to behave like this. Her small talk is an ironic reference to her first test when she was only allowed to talk about health and the weather. Now, however, it sounds natural. After greeting Higgins she ignores him and only addresses the Colonel. She thanks him for his kind, courteous behaviour towards her which gave her a sense of her own value and helped her to really become a lady. She then twists the knife even further by comparing Higgin's behaviour to her own as an uneducated flower girl and says that she learned her good manners *in spite of* him. Higgins's contribution, she says, was insignificant, because she could have learned the minor details of changing her appearance and speech from anyone. Higgins is furious and retorts that without him she would relapse within three weeks and finish up back in the gutter. Eliza's triumph is complete. Once again she has succeeded in enraging her teacher, but this time she herself remained calm. In a typical Shavian twist, her triumph does not last long. Just as she is protesting that she could not utter one of the old sounds even if she tried, her father appears. The shock is so great that she shouts out in her old way. Higgins is delighted.

The scene shows that Eliza has indeed learned more than her Pygmalion ever taught her. Now she treats Higgins as an equal. In fact, she is not only a match for him, but in some respects even superior. Qualities have come out in her which were previously disguised by her humble lifestyle. Higgins is so insensitive that he never noticed her potential and even now does not understand how much she has changed.

Eliza believes that the difference between a lady and a flower girl is not how she behaves, but how she is treated. This raises the basic theme of the play, namely, how to define social class. For if a flower girl can pass as a duchess because of her appearance and speech, it follows that anyone can move up into high society if they have the necessary energy and talent. By thus proving that class barriers are artificial Shaw is pleading for their removal. As a socialist he wanted everyone to be given a fair chance to make a decent living for themselves. He is saying that even the humblest members of society might have exceptional qualities and that society should find ways of enabling them to fulfil their potential and not hinder them by artificial class barriers. Higgins seems to be one of those who judge people by their appearance and manners. To him, being a lady is a question of pronunciation, grammar and clothes. Eliza, on the other hand, seems to define a lady as someone who respects herself and also has the respect of others.

The conversation between Eliza, Higgins and Pickering is prevented from becoming too heavy by Doolittle's explanation that he is dressed up because he is about to be married to Eliza's step-mother. This is another consequence of his falling a victim to middle class morality. He feels pressurised into doing what is expected of him. Everyone is invited to the wedding and when they go off to get ready Eliza and Higgins are left alone. Henry tries to persuade her to return home with him. He admits that he would miss her if she left, but when she does not respond immediately he becomes impatient. He refuses to go beyond a certain point in his attempt at a reconciliation. He will not, for instance, agree to treat her any differently, nor will he admit to any affection for her. His statement that he treats everyone alike and will not change for anyone might sound democratic, but is really an excuse for his egotism and makes him feel justified in being rude to everybody. He refuses to take the trouble to consider other people's feelings. He also makes it clear that his work is more important to him than anyone, including Eliza.

This is unacceptable to Eliza, who now values her independence too much to revert to their former relationship. She will no longer allow him to ignore her and demands to be treated with respect. This is the point where Pygmalion's 'statue' finally comes to life. But in a typically Shavian twist Eliza refuses to remain someone else's creation. For Shaw, one of the worst things that can happen to a person is to be intimidated and manipulated by other people. So by making his Galatea rebel he is warning against trying to make other people fit our own images of them.

When Eliza tells Higgins that Freddy is in love with her and has been writing to her regularly Higgins seems to be jealous. But it soon becomes clear that it is only because he does not want to see his 'creation' wasted. He has put so much effort into her training that she would now be fit to marry a king. Eliza then suggests that she could earn her living by teaching phonetics and could offer her services to Nepommuck. At this Higgins becomes furious and once more Eliza has the satisfaction of provoking him to anger. Suddenly, Higgins realises just how much the flower girl has changed. He had not noticed that whilst learning to speak, dress and behave like a lady her whole personality had developed. The stage direction 'Wondering at her' shows his surprise and admiration when he realises that she can now stand up to him. He actually prefers this kind of behaviour to her previous appeals for affection. Here Higgins is speaking as Shaw's mouthpiece, for it is well known that Shaw wanted men and women to be equal partners.

But Higgins wants Eliza back on his own terms. He would like her to go on helping him run his life and would enjoy her companionship, but refuses to give anything in return. It would be too much trouble to have to consider her feelings and needs. He would simply go on as before, devoting himself to his work and having Eliza in the background, there whenever he needed her. The play ends with Higgins giving Eliza orders about some shopping. These instructions, also the way he for-

mulates them, shows that he has not understood anything she said. He is too self-centred and conceited to
be able to respect another person. His behaviour also
contradicts his praise of her new strength of character
a few moments earlier.

The ending is left open. Higgins and Eliza are now
equally matched and, although they like each other,
neither will give in. In the final scene Eliza and Mrs Higgins go off to Doolittle's wedding, leaving Higgins laughing at the idea of her marrying Freddy. He is confident
that she will return, with the shopping, just as she has
always done. He is still incapable of seeing her as a person in her own right and not merely as his work of art.
Like the Greek Pygmalion, Higgins has created a new
woman, or rather has helped to create one, because
Eliza contributed quite a lot herself. But whereas his
Greek counterpart could not be happy until his statue
was given a soul, Higgins is unable to regard Eliza as
someone with a life and feelings of her own. Shaw's
Pygmalion is incapable of falling in love at all. There is
another, ironic way in which Shaw changes the legend.
For whereas the original Pygmalion brings his statue to
life by the power of love, Higgins begins by reducing a
living person to something more like a robot. However,
his 'statue' refuses to remain inanimate, but rebels
against her creator and becomes independent of him.

This last act would surprise and disappoint Shaw's
audience, who were used to traditional romances in
which love overcomes all obstacles, including class
barriers. Had not Shaw promised them such a cosy,
happy ending by giving his play the subtitle 'A Romance'? And did not he encourage them to expect the
traditional type of plot by reminding them of both the
Greek legend and the *Cinderella* fairy tale? But Shaw
would not be Shaw if he did not disappoint such expectations and refuse to romanticise. Anyone who has cor-

rectly interpreted the characters of Higgins and Eliza will understand that there can be no romantic ending, at least not between these two. The ambiguous ending is typical of Shaw's refusal to let his audience believe in fairy-tale solutions. Instead, he forces them to look at life realistically. The unexpected ending is intended to make audiences reject comfortable, unrealistic attitudes and really start thinking about the problems confronting people like Eliza, both as a flower girl and a genteel, but impoverished lady. Shaw probably believed that what Eliza actually does next is not so important. The main thing is that she is now more aware of herself and more in control of her own life. Shaw felt that people should always try to discover their own true nature and realise their own potential and this is what Eliza has achieved.

SEQUEL

The critics and general public were not happy with Shaw's ending and insisted on knowing what happened to Eliza. Producers and actors even sabotaged the author's intentions by suggesting a happy ending, for instance by Higgins throwing a rose after Eliza when she left for the wedding. So, reluctantly, Shaw added a sequel.

In this sequel Shaw points out how unlikely it is that Eliza would marry Higgins. In fact she marries Freddy and they open a small flower shop in a railway station arcade. Shaw makes a final comment on the class system by explaining that Freddy's upper class education and background has not equipped him for earning a living and that he has no idea how to handle money. After initial difficulties and much financial help from Colonel Pickering the business finally becomes a success. Eliza often visits Wimpole Street and helps to run the household. From the time when she established a different relationship with Higgins she began to nag him, although she never nags her husband or the Colonel, whom she loves as a father. She snaps at her former teacher on the slightest provocation and he no longer dares to tease her. He still has outbursts of anger and tries to bully her, but she stands up to him so ruthlessly that Pickering even has to ask her to treat him more kindly.

Doolittle becomes very popular with the aristocracy because of his down-to-earth manner. Politicians even ask his advice. Clara changes very radically. She was deeply shocked when she found out how she was taken in by Eliza. Also, the discovery that a girl of her own age could change so much in so short a time made her start thinking about her own life. When she realised that she had allowed her life to be governed by other people's standards she gave up her social pretentions. She became converted to Socialism and eventually got a job in a shop. So, like her brother, Freddy, she finally manages to earn her own living instead of trying to keep up the pretence of a life of luxury, which they cannot afford. Through Clara's development Shaw tried to persuade his audience that people can free themselves from inhibiting conventions and that they should take an honest, realistic look at their own lives.

The Characters

ELIZA DOOLITTLE ✓

Before she is transformed into a 'duchess' Eliza is generally known as Liza. When she first appears she is selling flowers late at night in London's Covent Garden vegetable market. She is about eighteen, poorly dressed and rather dirty. When a young man bumps into her and knocks her basket out of her hands Liza feels that she is justified in asking his obviously wealthy mother for compensation. This shows that she is not in awe of those with a higher social status. She seems to be a natural, direct sort of person.

Liza is very distressed when she is told that a man (Professor Higgins) is writing down every word she says. She insists that she is 'respectable' and has done nothing wrong. She obviously has a lot of self-respect. However, Liza repeats her protestations that she is only 'a poor girl' so often that we begin to suspect that she is deliberately exaggerating. There is another hint that she is perhaps not as helpless as she claims when she is caught lying. When she begs Pickering to buy a flower because 'I'm short for my lodgings' Higgins realises that she had lied a few moments before: 'Liar. You said you could change half-a-crown.' As soon as she has a little money in her purse we see a new side of her – cheeky and proud.

When Liza sees how much money Higgins has thrown to her she howls with delight and spends some of it on the luxury of riding home in a taxi. Hiring the taxi is her triumph over her poverty, however temporary. It shows that she has imagination and ambition. She would try to improve her life if she could. The taxi driver admires her spirit. Lying in bed that night in her cold, miserable room, Liza plans what to do with her new riches. Suddenly, a door to another world has been opened.

Liza shows initiative and determination in the way she seizes her opportunity. She knows that what Higgins said is true, that the way she speaks 'will keep her in the gutter to the end of her days'. So she decides to use the money for elocution lessons which will enable her to 'talk like a lady' and get a job in a flower shop. Her determination is so strong that she is able to stand Higgins' insults.

Liza is a quick, intelligent and talented pupil. Higgins and Pickering tell Mrs Higgins that they are amazed at how quickly she learns. Not only is she extremely good at imitating sounds, but she also learns to play the piano in a very short time.

At first her new position goes to her head and she becomes snobbish. She wants to show off in front of the girls she used to work with. She now judges them by their social position and finds them beneath her.

Liza is such a good and hard-working pupil that she easily passes the test. At the Embassy reception she is even taken for a princess. But then she realises what position she is in now that the experiment is over. She is in despair when she sees how she has been used and that she will now be discarded. We see how much she values her independence when she accuses Higgins of taking it away from her. Now she is in the humiliating position of being dependent on others for her food, clothes and somewhere to live.

Higgins has not noticed how Liza's personality has developed over the past six months. Not only has she learned a new way of speaking, she has also become more self-confident. She is no longer willing to let Higgins bully her and treat her as an inferior. She states her own terms for remaining with him and when he rejects them she refuses to stay. Eventually Higgins is forced to recognise that she has changed. He sees that she has become a much stronger person. She is more conscious of her own value and has more will-power than before. She has also become more dignified and graceful. Whereas Higgins only gave her the outer appearance of a lady, she now really does behave like one. Her gentility has become an integral part of her personality.

Eliza herself says that she began to value herself more when Colonel Pickering treated her with respect, 'That was the beginning of self-respect for me ... the difference between a lady and a flower girl is not how she behaves, but how she's treated'. At the end of the play Liza is able to define being a lady in complex psychological terms. She understands that true gentility is much more than outer appearance and a certain way of speaking.

The link between language and thought is shown by a comparison of Liza's speech at the beginning of the play and at the end. In Acts 1 and 2 she often expresses strong feelings by inarticulate howls. She is not capable of expressing them through language. By the end of the play, however, she has become very articulate and no longer needs to howl. Not only has she learned a whole new vocabulary, but she also understands herself better. For without understanding her own feelings she would not be able to express them so coherently.

At the end the roles of Eliza and Higgins have been reversed. Whereas she used to be completely dependent on him, now it is the professor who depends on his former pupil. He says that he needs her to help him organise his life, but we are not sure in how far he is also emotionally dependent on her. At the end it is Eliza who is in control of the situation, not Higgins. She is able to choose whether to go back with him or not. In his sequel Shaw explains that Liza eventually marries Freddy, but that she often visits Higgins and Pickering. She dominates and bullies Higgins, who does not dare to oppose her. Although Eliza is exposed as a fake, she still manages to retain a certain amount of social standing. The flower shop which she and Freddy open finally makes a profit and she herself even becomes something of a show-off.

PROFESSOR HENRY HIGGINS

Henry Higgins, a professor of phonetics, is nearly forty years old and a confirmed bachelor. Besides his own research on language he teaches the newly rich to speak more correctly so that they can increase their social prestige. As a scholar he is brilliant and can tell where people come from simply by the way they speak. He loves his work and lives for nothing else.

Although Higgins comes from a good family he has no manners. He is arrogant, rude, swears and completely ignores social conventions. He obviously feels superior to other people and yet he is no snob, for he is rude to everyone, regardless of their social status. His mother refuses to let him meet her friends because of his bad manners. Her son is so self-centred that he always says what he thinks without considering other people's feelings. Furthermore, he cannot even understand why anyone should be offended. He is genuinely surprised at people's reactions and tells his mother that he never intends to hurt their feelings. In fact, he is so egotistic that he never considers other people at all, not even to deliberately offend them.

Higgins's disdain of convention and hatred of pretentiousness reflect the author's own attitude to what he saw as empty rituals whose only purpose was to reinforce the barriers between the social classes. Yet whilst

Shaw is certainly using the professor to expose the falseness of these conventions, at the same time he is warning that any principle, if taken too far, becomes ridiculous. Higgins's refusal to make the slightest concession to social norms makes him unacceptable to everyone, regardless of their social class.

Higgins not only offends people by his outspokenness and disregard for social conventions, but also by his lack of understanding for others. For instance, when Pickering rebukes him for ignoring Eliza's feelings in Act 2, Henry replies that she has no feelings which they need bother about. Both Mrs Pearce and Mrs Higgins warn Henry that he is behaving irresponsibly towards Eliza, but he is so insensitive that he does not even understand the problem. When asked what is to become of her after the experiment, he callously suggests that they can just throw her back into the gutter.

Henry is so rude that Liza cannot learn good manners from him. It is ironic that although he trains her to move in high society, he himself is incapable of doing this. Besides his mother, Mrs Pearce also constantly reproaches the professor about his table-manners, untidiness and swearing.

Higgins is a teacher, but in a very limited sense, for he can only improve Liza's pronunciation, vocabulary and grammar. He does not realise that language is much more than a collection of sounds, words and sentences, but that it involves a person's whole being. He starts off a process in Eliza which he is later unable to control and is surprised when she develops in a way he did not foresee.

Higgins only appears to be interested in other human beings if he can make use of them for his phonetic experiments. He did not take on the bet out of pity for Liza, to help her to improve her life, but only to show off his own skills, to show how much he can do with unpromising material. After he has won the bet his behaviour towards Eliza is shameful. He not only fails to thank her, but completely ignores her and takes all the credit for himself. He does not realise how hard she has worked. He makes her feel that she has served her purpose and that he is no longer interested in her. When Eliza realizes how she has been exploited she accuses him of manipulating her in an irresponsible way.

In fact, Higgins did not deliberately manipulate Eliza. He simply did not think about her as a person. The experiment fascinated him to such an extent that he did not stop to think of any possible consequences. Again, as with his disdain for social conventions, Shaw is warning that something which might be positive in itself can be dangerous if taken to an extreme. In themselves, Higgins's passion for his work and his tremendous energy are admirable qualities. He really loves the English language and is genuinely distressed to hear it spoken badly. In fact, the only time he ever shows any sensitivity is when he talks about the language. We can almost believe that he is truly concerned about the plight of the underprivileged when he tells Pickering that Liza's accent will 'keep her in the gutter till the end of her days'. Unfortunately, however, he is so obsessed by the scientific aspect of his work that the social one becomes overlaid. Although we may admire him as a linguistic genius and find his enthusiasm endearing, at the same time we deplore his self-centredness and childish behaviour. Shaw seems to be suggesting that his skills do not compensate for his lack of human qualities.

Higgins not only lacks sensitivity towards other people, he is also incapable of understanding his own nature. He is full of contradictions. The image which he has of himself is that of an intellectual who is only concerned with the higher things in life – science, literature, classical music, philosophy and art. He prides himself on having a purely scientific mind and being in complete control of his emotions. However, this image is often contradicted – very entertainingly – by his childish, impulsive behaviour. At his mother's, for instance, he behaves like a spoilt child when he is forced to make polite conversation with people he dislikes. He also frequently bullies others, especially Liza. She recognises this contradiction, accusing him of being 'a cruel tyrant ... nothing but a bully'. Higgins describes himself as a 'shy, diffident sort of man' with irreproachable manners. But in fact, he is just the opposite: a tyrannical egotist, rude and with no consideration whatever for other people. He protests that he never swears, but just after Mrs Pearce has rebuked him for swearing he loses his temper and swears again. Although he says he hardly ever loses his temper, he actually loses it several times during the play. Yet his anger never lasts long. He is not the sort of person to bear grudges. Indeed, he is completely free of small-minded, petty thoughts, which is why he is so hurt by Eliza's suggestion that he might sometime accuse her of stealing the jewels and clothes which he gave her.

These contradictions do not mean that Henry is a hypocrite. He is simply so arrogant that he cannot believe he ever does anything wrong. So whenever anyone accuses him of bad behaviour he always tries to find an excuse. Henry is a prime example of Shaw's use of irony and paradox. He prides himself on his brilliant mind, but constantly shows how little he understands about himself, other people or life in general.

It is the contradictions in Higgins's character which prevent us from regarding him as a despicable, heartless brute. We are also prepared to forgive him his faults because he is so witty and entertaining. Although the audience is encouraged to think seriously about his irresponsible behaviour, at the same time they will not judge him too harshly. The impression Higgins gives is that of a well-intentioned, but misguided genius, whose passion for his life's work blinds him to everything else.

At the end of the play Higgins has not only taught Liza to speak like a lady, but he has also, unintentionally, helped her to discover her own personality. Whereas he starts off as the more dominant of the two, at the end it is Eliza who is the more powerful figure. In contrast to Liza's new self-awareness, Higgins hardly changes at all. He still lacks self-knowledge and does not see the contradictions within himself, nor does he understand that his behaviour was irresponsible. Eventually he learns to value Liza's personality, which is an improvement on his unfeeling, stereotyped judgement of her at the beginning. But he never becomes emotionally mature, as she does. He is too fixed in his ways, too empty emotionally to be able to make any kind of compromise and to adapt to her new attitudes. He wants her to return on his terms or not at all.

Higgins's description of the way he sees their future relationship is another example of the contradictions in his own nature and of his lack of self-knowledge. He would like Eliza as a consort, a companion, but the way he continues to treat her, especially his final remarks, show that he cannot change his attitude towards her. He will always see himself as her teacher and she will always be his creation. He does not seem to feel any real affection for her, but simply finds it convenient to have her around.

ALFRED DOOLITTLE ✓

Alfred Doolittle, Liza's father, is a dustman. He first appears dressed in his working clothes. Shaw describes him as 'elderly but vigorous' with an interesting face and apparently 'free from fear and conscience'. He has a 'remarkably expressive voice', which reflects his habit of always expressing his emotions freely. He has a roguish, vital personality.

Alfred is not a realistic character, but a caricature. It is very unlikely that a dustman would be either so philosophical or so articulate. He is a wonderful talker. Higgins immediately recognises this and says that if he had elocution lessons, in three months time he could become a member of Parliament or a clergyman.

Doolittle has many faults. He is a lazy drunkard and used to beat Liza, his illegitimate daughter. He has neglected her, allowing her to make her own living as best she could. She was so poor that she had to wear rags and live in squalor. Then, as soon as he sees the possibility of making money out of her, he tries to black-mail Higgins and eventually sells her for five pounds. He never shows any interest in her and does not care what happens to her. Liza herself never wants to see him again.

Yet, despite his faults, Doolittle is a likeable character. His paradoxical arguments are witty, original and entertaining. And he is so frank about his amorality and selfishness that the audience tends to laugh *with* him rather than *at* him.

Doolittle's main function in the play is to act as a mouthpiece for the author's own ideas. Shaw uses him to provoke his audience into rethinking their conventional views on morality. Besides having an illegitimate daughter, Doolittle challenges traditional ideas about marriage by living with a woman who is not his wife. Although he is willing to marry her, she refuses because the present insecure situation forces Alfred to treat her better than if they were married. Doolittle consciously violates bourgeois morality, which was also the moral code of the audience. For instance, instead of working hard and saving money, his aim in life is to do as little work as possible and enjoy himself as much as he can. His name, 'do little', expresses his laziness. Although he is actually a navvy, or unskilled labourer, he prefers to work as a dustman because it is easier. He explains that he is one of the 'undeserving' poor. This, too, is a rejection of bourgeois values, for the Victorians believed that people should only be given help if they 'deserved' it in some way, for example if they were trying hard to make a living but were not succeeding. Doolittle freely admits that he does not fit into this category because he never really tries to improve his life.

Alfred's appearance as a gentleman in the second half of the play is a surprising contrast to his former appearance. The paradox that he is now miserable, not happy, is comical because it is so unexpected. As a joke, Higgins had written to an American millionaire, praising Doolittle as the most original moralist in England. When the millionaire died he left Alfred a large annual income on condition that he gave lectures in support of moral reform. This is a typical Shavian paradox, because, ironically, a man who used to be completely amoral is now supposed to persuade others to live by bourgeois norms and values. Whereas previously he could ignore social conventions, now he has been pushed up into the middle class and feels pressurised to conform to their norms of respectability.

He feels defeated and trapped, besieged by relatives and intimidated by money and middle class morality. He has lost the freedom to live as he chooses and to make his own decisions. Yet, although he dislikes his new position, he can cope with it. He is accepted and liked for his natural vitality and personality.

Doolittle's rise forms a comic parallel to his daughter's development. As she becomes a lady, he turns into a 'gentleman'. But with him it is only superficial. He learns neither a new way of speaking nor of thinking. He only dresses differently and accepts the conventions of the class to which he now belongs. Liza's transformation, on the other hand, is exactly the opposite. At first she only changes superficially as she puts on new clothes and learns a new way of speaking. But then she is transformed in a deeper, more permanent sense. Whereas Alfred resignes himself to his fate, Eliza gains more freedom to choose how she wants to live. Both illustrate the risks involved in moving up in society and show that social improvement does not necessarily bring happiness.

COLONEL PICKERING

Pickering and Higgins are both interested in phonetics and both are bachelors. But otherwise they are opposites. Whereas Higgins is an egotist to whom social conventions are unimportant, Pickering is the perfect gentleman. Indeed, his correct behaviour makes him seem a little old-fashioned and conservative. He is more reserved about the experiment than Higgins and feels some responsibility towards Liza. Before they start he asks Henry if he has a good reputation as far as women are concerned. And later he rebukes his friend for his rudeness towards the girl. At times, however, his enthusiasm for the experiment overlays his conscience, such as when he and his friend describe it to Mrs Higgins.

Pickering is always polite to Liza and addresses her as Miss Doolittle. His politeness is not just good manners, but expresses a genuine respect for other people. During the experiment he supports and encourages Liza, acting as a mediator between pupil and teacher. He understands Liza's need for praise and encouragement. It is possible that without the Colonel's help Liza would have given up. After the experiment is over he continues to support her by helping her and Freddy to run a flower shop.

Pickering is a dramatic foil to Higgins. His generosity, calmness and gentlemanly behaviour show up Higgins's selfishness, excitability and rudeness all the more clearly. Like Mrs Pearce and Henry's mother, he represents the common-sense view. He also fulfils a similar function to Higgins's mother in that he adds a new dimension to Higgins: if a decent, humane man like the Colonel is the professor's friend, then there must be something likeable about him.

MRS PEARCE

Mrs Pearce, Higgins's housekeeper, is a respectable, sensible and practical woman. She treats her employer like a small boy who needs looking after. She shows sympathy for Liza, although she calls her a 'foolish ignorant girl', a 'silly girl' and a 'child'. Her social status is higher than Liza's, but she is not snobbish or condescending towards her. She rebukes Higgins for his irresponsible attitude towards the girl.

Mrs Pearce's dramatic function, like that of Pickering and Mrs Higgins, is to represent the practical, responsible way of looking at the experiment.

MRS HIGGINS

Mrs Higgins, Henry's mother, is a woman of great character. She is intelligent, charming, dignified and wealthy. She is the ideal mother, wise, tolerant, understanding and caring. Yet she is also independent. She leads a quiet, contented, orderly life. Her room expresses her personality and also her sense of beauty. She is understanding and accepts people as they are. In difficult situations she is the one who remains calm and takes control of the situation. With her around we feel that nothing can go seriously wrong.

Although Mrs Higgins's son is so famous, she still treats him like a naughty child, rebuking him for his bad manners and thoughtlessness. She knows how ambitious he is and sympathises with Liza, whom he has reduced to the object of his experiments. Like Mrs Pearce she wonders what is to become of the girl later on and is horrified that neither Henry nor Pickering can see this problem. After the quarrel between Eliza and Higgins it is Mrs Higgins who offers Eliza shelter and takes her side.

Mrs Higgins is a minor character, but she is important to the story for various reasons. From a practical point of view she is useful because Henry can use her home to introduce Liza into polite society. In Act 5 she acts as a mediator between Higgins and Eliza when she tries to explain to her son where he went wrong. Furthermore, she provides a role model for Eliza in her new surroundings.

Mrs Higgins provides a dramatic foil to her son. By contrast with his mother Higgins's faults stand out more clearly. She is a polite, sensitive person who responds to appeals for help and gives good advice when it is needed.

The introduction of Higgins's mother adds a new dimension to the professor. He becomes more human as we get to know him not only as a scientist, but also as someone's son. Her behaviour towards him suggests that we should not take him too seriously, for he has his faults.

Mrs Higgins also shares Mrs Pearce's function of expressing the common-sense, responsible view of the whole experiment.

THE EYNSFORD HILLS

In Shaw's day the upper and upper middle classes firmly believed in rigid class distinctions. Those with inherited wealth, like the Eynsford Hills, felt superior to those who earned their living in business or 'trade', as they called it. Even families such as the Eynsford Hills, who could no longer afford a life of luxury, did not think of training the children to go out to work. At most, the sons might be educated for the church or careers in law. Instead, they tried to live like the upper class and spent their time attending concerts, the theatre, 'at-home' afternoons and formal receptions.

The problem of Eliza's future is personified by the Eynsford Hills. The mother feels she has to keep up a facade which she cannot really afford. In fact, they have become social misfits. They have just enough to live on, but not enough to be able to mix with fashionable society. They are living on the fringe of the wealthier classes. Yet going out to earn a living would be beneath them. Shaw directs his satire at such people. As a social reformer he constantly attacked the snobbery and insensitivity of the upper and upper middle classes and forced them to take notice of society's problems.

Shaw also mocks the Eynsford Hills for letting social conventions rule their lives. They embody the middle class morality which Doolittle finds so oppressive. Like Mrs Eynsford Hill, Alfred eventually surrenders his personal freedom to a bourgeois life style.

Mrs Eynsford Hill

Mrs Eynsford Hill is a respectable gentlewoman who can no longer afford an upper class life style. She suffers from the fact that she cannot give her son and daughter the usual advantages of the upper class. And yet she cannot free herself from the social conventions which make her so unhappy.

Clara

Clara is a pathetic, ridiculous figure. She does not seem to realise that the family is no longer either rich or respected, but still treats others as if they were beneath her. Shaw mocks her by exposing her stupidity and gullibility. At the beginning of the play Clara sees Liza as a flower girl and treats her with her usual arrogance and rudeness. When she meets her again at Mrs Higgins's at-home afternoon, she does not recognise her. But Clara is very easily influenced and quickly becomes one of Eliza's most fervent admirers. Eager to be thought up to date, she even imitates Eliza, which, of course, shocks her mother.

Clara is one of Shaw's instruments for attacking class barriers. For if high society thinks a flower girl is a duchess simply because of her appearance and speech then their standards must be artificial.

Besides her function as a representative of the upper class, Clara is also a dramatic foil to Eliza. Her rudeness and arrogance form a sharp contrast to Eliza's natural good manners and sensitivity. This again raises the question of what is really meant by aristocratic, or ladylike behaviour. In his sequel Shaw explains how Clara develops. She shows remarkable strength and spirit by eventually rejecting the social conventions of her class and going out to earn her own living.

Freddy

Freddy is an uncomplicated, good-hearted, easygoing young man. He is weak and easily influenced and falls in love with Eliza at first sight. However, he is mediocre. His failure to find a taxi in the first scene is an indication of his general uselessness. Shaw informs us in his sequel that when Freddy and Eliza are planning to open a flower shop, Colonel Pickering has to lend him money and explain what a cheque book and a bank account are. Yet he manages to free himself from the bourgeois norms which inhibit his mother. Like Eliza, he has enough personal freedom to be able to cope with his new social position.

Themes

As a socialist Shaw was deeply unhappy about the injustices of industrial society in nineteenth century Britain. Wages were too low to provide a minimum standard of living, young children worked in factories and mines and there was very little decent housing or sanitation for working people. He decided to write plays in order to draw attention to the state of society. In the preface to *Pygmalion* he said that it was meant to teach the audience, but that this did not prevent it from being enjoyable. He was convinced that great art must teach and felt that plays could not be important unless they dealt with some aspect of contemporary life. By setting *Pygmalion* in contemporary London he invited the audience to apply its messages to their own society. He hoped that they would recognise the tremendous gulf between the social classes and also the inequalities between men and women.

In *Pygmalion* Shaw examined the following aspects of the problem of social inequality.

1. THE LINK BETWEEN LANGUAGE AND SOCIAL CLASS

Shaw explained in the preface to *Pygmalion* that the way people speak reveals their background: 'it is impossible for an Englishman to open his mouth without making some other Englishman despise him'. He realised that some people had "accents that cut them off from all high employment". His heroine, Eliza Doolittle, is one of these people. When Higgins meets her in the market he tells Pickering that her accent will 'keep her in the gutter till the end of her days'. Shaw has chosen dialect to illustrate the snobbishness and rigidity of the contemporary British class system. Eliza's progress demonstrates how a socially unacceptable accent can be changed into one with more prestige in order to improve her chances in life. The implication is that society would be more equal if 'low' dialects could be eradicated. Shaw felt that his role was to provoke people into thinking about things, not to give them ready-made answers. So we do not actually know if he really supported this idea or not.

Liza's transformation also raises the question of the role of language in revealing and even forming a person's character. For at the end of the play Eliza is able to express herself in a much more differentiated way than at the beginning, when strong emotions often came out as an inarticulate howl. This suggests that she now understands her own feelings much better.

2. DEFINING SOCIAL CLASS

In Shaw's society the upper and upper middle classes led comfortable, even luxurious lives. They insisted on rigid class barriers in order to protect their own privileged position. In *Pygmalion* Shaw suggests that if high society thinks a flower seller is a duchess or princess simply because of her appearance and speech, then these social distinctions must be empty and artificial. If a flower girl can, to all appearances, be turned into a duchess in six months, then the only difference is that a duchess has inherited more social prestige and money. The differences between people, then, are social, not natural. Eliza is just as intelligent as those with a higher social position, but it is hidden by her poverty. With the proper training she is able to fulfil her potential and shows that she is quick to learn and has a mind of her own.

To Shaw social class seems to be a question of character, speech and manners rather than of birth. He implies that with the necessary training anyone with enough will-power and ability can, like Liza, improve their social status. He warns, though, that the transformation is not a superficial one, but involves the whole personality and results in a complete reorientation. The message is that it is only the lack of education and opportunity which causes the Lizas of this world to remain deprived. Shaw is warning that Liza's potential would normally be stifled by a class system which is so rigid that it would condemn her to a life in the gutter. He is arguing that the class system should become more flexible.

Through *Pygmalion* Shaw told his audience that good breeding does not come automatically to those born into respectable families. Neither Higgins nor Clara fit the traditional definition of 'genteel', despite their backgrounds. Shaw even seems to be implying that the common people are really more aristocratic in their nature than those born into high society. For Liza, an uneducated, working class flower seller, has natural good manners and sensitivity.

The classes who regard background and wealth as important are presented as dishonest towards themselves. In the play they are represented by the Eynsford Hills. Shaw mocks their snobbish social pretensions and suggests that they allow rigid conventions and bourgeois morality to rule their lives. For, although the family is in financial difficulties, they feel it would be beneath them to go out and work for a living. Their desperate attempts to keep up appearances make them more pathetic than if they were to face up to their situation honestly and realistically.

3. EDUCATION AND SOCIAL CLASS

Shaw makes us wonder what education really means. For the success of Higgins's experiment proves that people can be changed considerably by education. Eliza's exceptional qualities were hidden because of the kind of life she was forced to lead and the educational system failed to help her.

4. ILLUSIONS:
MYTH AND FAIRY STORY

The Pygmalion myth

Shaw's drama is based on a Greek myth about *Pygmalion,* a sculptor and ruler of Cyprus. He was so repelled by the faults of real life women that he decided to sculpt a perfect one in ivory. He dressed the statue and put jewelry on it. But then he fell in love with it and prayed to the goddess of love to give it life. His prayer was answered, Pygmalion's dreams were fulfilled and he married his ideal woman, who was then called Galatea.

In Shaw's play Professor Higgins is Pygmalion and Eliza Doolittle the woman he creates and gives life to. The stories are very similar in that neither Pygmalion nor Higgins get on very well with women, both create a new woman and both dress their 'creations' in beautiful clothes and jewelry. However, Higgins's aim is different from Pygmalion's. He does not want to create an ideal woman, but is only interested in demonstrating his own skills. In fact, he does not seem to need other people at all and seems incapable of loving anyone.

It is typical of Shaw that he gives the legend a twist. Instead of fulfilling the audience's expectations of a happy ending, he makes his heroine turn against her creator. Whereas Galatea is brought to life in answer to her creator's prayers, Liza develops in a way Higgins did not foresee. In fact, Higgins did not so much create her as uncover something which was already there. For her beauty and natural dignity were obscured by the kind of life she was forced to lead in Covent Garden. Her exceptional talents only needed to be uncovered and guided into certain channels, just as Pygmalion's statue needed to be given life by its creator. When Eliza finally achieves her full potential she suddenly realises how Higgins has exploited her. She refuses to remain his creation and even rejects him. She insists on 'coming to life' in her own way. Finally, Higgins realises what a splendid human being lay hidden under the exterior of the simple flower girl. In many respects she is now his superior because she is a warmer and more complete human being. But he is incapable of adapting to the changes in her and refuses to treat her as an equal. He will never see her as anything but his creation. Liza rejects this role and eventually forces him to accept her on equal terms, as we find out from the sequel.

The Cinderella theme

The story of Eliza Doolittle is a variation on the familiar 'from rags to riches' tale. One of the best known examples is the fairy story *Cinderella* ('Aschenputtel') in which a poor, dirty, badly treated, but beautiful girl is turned into a princess and is rewarded with the love of a prince. This type of romantic story may provide some comfort to ordinary people because it suggests that the same thing could happen to anyone.

It is typical of Shaw that he uses such a familiar story to arouse certain expectations, then gives it an ironic twist. Audiences would certainly be lured into thinking that they were watching a variation of the fairy tale: in both cases the girl attends a high society event, in Cinderella's case a ball and in Eliza's an embassy reception. Both are taken for princesses. Towards the end of the ball Cinderella runs away, losing her glass slipper as she goes. Eliza, too, runs away from Higgins's house after they return home from the reception. With Cinderella the lost slipper is the means of bringing her and her prince together. (He fell in love with her at the ball, found the slipper and went looking for its owner). Shaw also includes the element of a slipper, but not as a symbol of love. After the reception Eliza throws Higgins's slipper at him in a gesture of anger and rejection, an action which contradicts previous comparisons with *Cinderella*. In *Pygmalion* the slippers are rather a symbol of man's domination over woman, as Eliza fetches them for her teacher.

Whereas the fairy tale has a happy ending, Shaw's drama is much more realistic. He refuses to indulge his audience's romantic longings, but makes them face up to the fact that problems are not magically solved with the climax. The audience is forced to think about what would happen to Eliza in the real world and to think about the type of society which condemns people like her to a life of misery.

The contrast with Shaw's more realistic versions of both the myth and the fairy tale would surprise the audience. Shaw wanted to provoke them into rethinking their attitudes to stereotyped, conventional plots. By showing them a different way of looking at things he tried to persuade them to reject illusions and look at life more realistically.

5. FEMINISM, EQUALITY AND SOCIAL CONVENTIONS

In Shaw's day women were not treated as persons in their own right, but as the property of fathers and husbands. Doolittle is a typical example of this attitude. He not only beats his daughter, but also feels justified in selling her to Higgins, since she is quite clearly his property. Middle and upper middle class women were not expected to go out to work, but to stay at home and look after their husbands so that they would be able to cope with the outside world. The moral code, however, was hypocritical, demanding that women be chaste, but allowing men sexual freedom. Many women were beginning to rebel against the domination of men over women and were campaigning for the right to vote. This meant demonstrating in public, going on hunger strikes and being thrown into prison. Shaw strongly supported their movement, the suffragettes, and gave lectures for them. By the end of World War I, in 1918, the climate of opinion had changed so much that women easily won the right to vote. At first it was limited to women under 30, but later gradually extended.

Shaw used *Pygmalion* to attack the bourgeois idea that it was not 'respectable' for women to go out to work. This is partly expressed by Mrs Higgins at the end of Act 3, when she points out the disadvantages of being a respectable lady with a small income, like Mrs Eynsford Hill: 'The manners and habits that disqualify a lady from earning her own living'. Shaw also challenges conventional ideas on marriage when Higgins suggests that a wealthy husband might be found for Eliza. In a typical Shavian paradox he says that it is more immoral for a woman to look for a rich husband than to go out and earn her own living.

Through his plays Shaw told his audiences that they should not allow social conventions to rule their lives, but should think for themselves. He believed that this would contribute to making society more equal. He wanted the middle and upper classes to free themselves from their empty, fixed attitudes and conventions and the working class to try to improve their own lives. He constantly encouraged people to develop as much as possible and used *Pygmalion* to show how this could be done.

At first, when Liza goes to stay with Higgins, she is intimidated by him and by her new life. She accepts Higgins's treatment of her and even behaves like his servant, fetching his slippers and organising his life for him. It is as if she were trying to buy his affection. She does not develop completely until she finally asserts herself and refuses to be dominated any longer. By the end of the play she is at ease with her new lifestyle. In Shavian drama the worst thing that can happen to a person is to be intimidated by someone else, because this means being used and humiliated.

Shaw set himself up as a critic of the status quo, always in opposition, always rebelling. On principle, he always expressed unconventional points of view. He believed that rebellion was necessary if society and mankind was to make any progress. His attitude was a reaction against the complacency and conservatism of Victorian society. In all his works he tried to break down the rigid conventions of his society and to encourage free will and flexibility. He was an important bridge between the nineteenth and the twentieth centuries, helping his society to adapt to the tremendous changes which were being brought about by new technological and scientific developments.

6. SCIENCE

Shaw' society was going through a period of tremendous social change. One of the greatest upheavals was caused by Charles' Darwin who explained the evolutionary process in terms of natural selection. People found it extremely difficult to come to terms with this contradiction of the biblical interpretation of the world. Shaw was influenced by Darwin and felt that society could evolve into something better if it could adapt to the new circumstances. The greatest challenge were the new developments in industry and technology. It is against this background that we must see Shaw's constant warnings that society needs to free itself of conventional ways of thinking and react to changes with an open mind if it is to progress. In his dramas he tried to assert and strengthen free will, which he saw as an important means of adapting to new situations. He told his audiences that man is capable of shaping his own destiny.

Although Shaw was fascinated by the recent advances in science, he was worried by the scientist's lack of responsibility and warned against putting a blind faith in progress and science. This explains his criticism of Higgins's transformation of Liza into something resembling a talking robot. Although the experiment was successful, Higgins ignored the fact that he was dealing with a human being with feelings and a personality of her own. Shaw is warning that the scientist must behave responsibly and should not manipulate people in order to prove a point. He implies that scientists should not become so obsessed by their work that they forget how it affects other people or society in general.

Other Elements

SETTING/SYMBOLISM

The play is set in London at the beginning of the twentieth century. It begins late at night in Covent Garden vegetable market. It is raining hard and people are running for shelter. This beginning illustrates Shaw's symbolical use of the weather to underline meaning. The darkness, rain and general confusion reflect the darkness and chaos of Liza's life. She is living a hand-to-mouth life, unsure of where her next meal will come from and whether she will be able to pay her rent.

The weather is used again to give more significance to the meeting of Liza and Freddy. As he bumps into her, knocking her basket out of her hands, there is lightning and thunder. Shaw makes sure that the reader does not miss the point by explaining that the weather 'orchestrates' the incident. Later the importance of this meeting becomes clear, firstly because Freddy falls in love with her and secondly because with the money paid to compensate the loss of her flowers Liza begins to climb the social ladder. Then, as the tension of Act 1 gradually fades, the storm passes.

At the end of the play Liza can see things more clearly and has gained a sense of her own value as a person. The feeling that she is starting a new life is reinforced by the fact that when Higgins meets her at his mother's it is morning, the beginning of a new day. Besides the time of day, the setting also has a symbolic function. It is fitting that now Eliza is more in control of her own life she should be in Mrs Higgins's elegant, orderly drawing room. This is described in great detail at the beginning of Act 3. Shaw himself points out that it is very unlike her son's living room, which is crowded with furniture and scientific instruments and reflects the exactness and functional outlook of the scientist.

One of Shaw's main intentions when writing *Pygmalion* was to draw attention to the miserable conditions in which the working class were living. One way in which he did this was by describing their homes. In contrast to both Mrs Higgins's and her son's flats, Liza only has one rented room. It is in a poor area and is damp and cold, with a broken window. One detail of it, however, suggests that Liza has dreams of a better life, for on her wall are pictures of ladies' dresses, torn from newspapers. Liza's transformation from flower seller to lady is underlined by a symbolic change of name. As a flower girl she is generally known as Liza, but she is presented to high society as Eliza.

STAGE DIRECTIONS

At first English audiences were shocked by Shaw's plays. They were angry because he did not show the slightest respect for any of their beliefs or conventions. So theatre directors were unwilling to put them on stage. Because of these difficulties Shaw decided to try publishing them as books instead. In those days it was not usual to print dramas in book form. It had been done before, but they looked very unattractive and the authors did not try to help the reader to imagine the plays on stage. Shaw remedied this situation by including plenty of explanations and descriptions. To give the reader better value for money he even included prefaces to his plays, in which he explained what he was trying to say. In fact, his plays were read just as much for these prefaces as for the plays themselves. Before long, other playwrights copied him and gradually a large play-reading public was created.

Shaw's stage directions are indeed extremely detailed. At the beginning of the play, for example, he describes the scene in Covent Garden in the rain. Then, at the beginning of Acts 2 and 3, he gives lengthy descriptions of Higgins's and his mother's drawing rooms, respectively. Besides helping the reader to visualise the settings, Shaw also gave detailed descriptions of the characters – their appearance, the way they speak and their movements. The effect of such detail was to make the characters and events seem more real, so that people were more likely to be interested in them. For instance, many of the characters introduced in Act 1 are associated with various places which would be familiar to the readers or audience. This gives the impression that the play is about real people and takes place in the actual world. In fact, Shaw wanted the play to be as realistic as possible, which was something quite new in those days (see 'The Author and His Times').

Style

Pygmalion has been described as Shaw's most characteristic play. This is also true of its style. The clear, straightforward, lively language mirrors Shaw's way of thinking. He concentrates on what he wants to say, without dressing it up in elaborate vocabulary. This style suits Shaw's purpose of appealing to the head rather than the heart.

Although Shaw tried to make his audiences look at life realistically, the plays themselves are not realistic. They are full of unlikely events, coincidences and flat, caricature-like figures. He is more interested in using characters to put forward certain opinions than in presenting them as credible, rounded human beings. Nevertheless, he still manages to give them vivid personalities.

The characters' personalities are partly expressed by their accent and vocabulary. Liza, for example, speaks Cockney English and uses very colourful expressions, including slang. This is contrasted with the more formal style of her betters – Higgins, Pickering, Mrs Higgins, and the Eynsford Hills. Higgins's personality is revealed by his frequent swearing, spontaneous outbursts ('Oh, Lord knows!', 'What! That thing!', 'Oh Lord! What an evening! What a crew!') and use of the imperative to order people about ('Put her in the dustbin', 'Take her away at once', 'Put out the lights'). His images are very colourful ('crooning like a bilious pigeon', 'squashed cabbage leaf') and he is extremely witty ('Somebody is going to touch you, with a broomstick').

Personality is also expressed by the types of sentences people use. Higgins, for instance, often speaks in short sentences or exclamations. This reflects his erratic, impatient nature, and also his energy ('We'll start today: now! this moment!'). This emotional style forms an ironic contrast with his image of himself as a cool, distanced, objective scientist and philosopher.

Short sentences and phrases are also characteristic of Doolittle's speech. However, he makes a different impression from Higgins. This is partly because of the formal way he addresses others ('So help me, Governor; I never did') and partly because of the rhetorical devices which he uses. His speeches on 'undeserving poverty' in Act 2, for instance, are full of rhetorical questions ('What am I, Governors both? I ask you, what am I?'), his statements are balanced and contrasted ('I don't need less than a deserving man: I need more') and he repeats certain sentence patterns ('I don't need less ... I don't eat less ...'). Doolittle's deliberate, skillful way of speaking reveals his self-confidence and also gives him dignity. The paradox of his appearance as a dustman and his way of speaking produces a comic effect.

Doolittle illustrates Shaw's original combination of comedy and seriousness. For whilst the dustman's opinions are amusing, at the same time they challenged the audience's bourgeois virtues of hard work, respectability, thrift and responsibility. Indeed, to the conventional, puritanical Victorian mind Shaw's gaiety in itself was revolutionary. But he knew he could not persuade people to think about serious matters if he did not amuse them at the same time. His dramatic technique relied on paradox, irony and satire. He turned generally accepted 'truths' into their opposites in surprising and amusing ways in order to startle his audience into seeing new, unexpected possibilities.

Shaw chose comedy as his tool because it is irreverent and flexible. Nothing is sacred. It allowed him to expose empty conventions, hypocrisy and arrogance in many different situations. Sometimes the comedy is

light-hearted and farcical, sometimes ironic, even bitterly sarcastic, and sometimes tragicomic. Although
Doolittle is the most obviously comic figure, it is
Higgins who provides most of the humour. Sometimes
he amuses us with his verbal wit, slangy expressions
and strong, usually comic metaphors. Sometimes we
laugh at the ironic contrast between his image of himself as a 'shy, diffident sort of man' and his outbursts of
temper, rudeness and egotism. He also gives us some
situational comedy, for example when he visits his
mother and is so excited that he keeps bumping into
things. There are many other examples of situational
comedy throughout the play. For instance, when Liza's
astonishment at seeing her father makes her revert to
her Cockney accent after saying she could not utter any
of her old sounds even if she tried.

Form and Structure

Pygmalion is clearly structured, with a beginning, a middle and an end. It moves along quickly so that the audience is never bored. Interest is sustained by a great variety of scene and mood. Each Act is broken up into several smaller sections involving different groups of people. The first Act, for example, begins with the Eynsford Hills. Then there is the incident with Liza and Freddy. The bustle and excitement of the beginning gradually gives way to a calmer mood as Liza talks first to Pickering, then Higgins. Different types of scenes alternate with each other throughout the whole plot. Some scenes move the story along, whilst others are calmer and more concerned with certain themes.

Doolittle's two appearances are an example of this variety. At the two points when he appears the tone is quite serious. In Act 5, especially, the tension is very high. Doolittle provides comic relief and relieves the tension. He also revives the audience's interest. By interrupting the development of the plot Doolittle's appearances also encourage the audience to distance themselves from it, giving them time to think about what has gone before.

The scenes with Doolittle illustrate two important elements of the plot's structure – parallels and contrasts. For, like his daughter, he too rises in society. His first appearance as a dustman marks the beginning of Liza's rise; his second, as a wealthy gentleman, coincides with her triumph. On the first occasion he is surprised at the change in Liza's appearance, on the second she is surprised to see her father dressed as a gentleman. But the parallel also includes an element of paradox, for Doolittle's prosperous exterior hides his

spiritual defeat. This can be seen as a warning, under-
lining the emptiness of Liza's social success.

Further contrasts and parallels running through the
play are the discrepancies between the lives of the more
privileged social classes and the desperately poor; the
clash between conventional and unconventional norms
of behaviour and morality; the contrasts and parallels
between various characters and groups of characters,
and also the contrasts within single characters, such as
the old and the new Liza and Doolittle.

An interesting point in the structure of the plot is the
question of the climax. It could be argued that the climax is Liza's appearance at the embassy reception,
where she is taken for a princess. But Shaw does not regard this scene as important. He uses asterisks to signal that it could even be omitted. His explanation was
that 'the theatre could not afford its expense and it made
the play too long' (Meisel 1963, p. 172.). Shaw himself
reluctantly added the scene to the musical version, *My
Fair Lady*, as a concession to the audience's lack of
imagination. In the musical Liza's final test is the climax, but it is changed into a ball. Shaw was more interested in Liza's development and the conflict between
her and Higgins. The climax of *Pygmalion* could even be
narrowed down to Liza's despairing cry, 'Whats to become of me?' after the reception. Shaw found mental processes much more exciting than physical action. All his
plays centre on discussion and the clash of ideas and
opposing values.

Besides introducing a completely new type of play,
the play of ideas, Shaw departed from theatrical tradi-
tion by refusing to give his audiences the stereotyped,
predictable endings they were used to. Because he described *Pygmalion* as a 'Romance' and because of the
type of story they would expect a happy, romantic out-
come. But Shaw denied his audience the luxury of illu-

sion. Instead, he shows that Higgins is incapable of adapting to the new Eliza and that she is no longer willing to live on his terms and lets us draw our own conclusions as to what will happen next. The play ends in tension.

Bibliography

Text Edition

Shaw, George Bernard: *Pygmalion*. Penguin 1984 (Klettbuch 5738)

Selected Bibliography

Berst, Charles A.: *Bernard Shaw and the Art of Drama*. University of Illinois Press, Chicago & London 1973.

Brown, G. E.: *George Bernard Shaw*, Evans Brother Ltd., London 1970.

Meisel, M.: *Shaw and the Nineteenth-Century Theatre*. Princeton University Press 1963

Morgan, Margery M.: *The Shavian Playground*. Methuen, London 1972

Otten, K./Rohmann, G. (Hrsg.): *George Bernard Shaw*. Wissenschaftliche Buchgesellschaft, Darmstadt 1978

Solomon, Stanley J.: *Theme and Structure in Getting Married*, Shaw Review, V, 3, September 1962

Whitman, Robert F.: *Shaw and the Play of Ideas*. Cornell University Press, Ithaca & London 1977

Willy Russell
«Educating Rita»

Contents

The Author and His Times

Educating Rita is to a large degree autobiographical. Like Rita, William Martin Russell, born in 1947, was also brought up in a working class family. They lived on a housing estate just outside Liverpool. His father worked in a factory before buying a fish-and-chip shop and his mother had a job in a warehouse. His experience of school is mirrored in Rita's description on pp.23-24. He, too, shared his schoolmates' antipathy towards education and once described his school days in an interview:

When I was eleven they sent me to a secondary school in Huyton. Like all the other Knowsley kids I was frightened of Huyton. There were millions of new houses there and flats, and everyone said there were gangs with bike chains and broken bottles and truck spanners. What everyone said was right; playtime had nothing to do with play, it was about survival. Thugs roamed the concrete and casually destroyed anything that couldn't move fast enough. Dinner time was the same only four times as long. If you were lucky enough to survive the food itself then you had to get out into the playground world of protection rackets, tobacco hustlers, trainee contract killers and plain no-nonsense sadists. And that's without the teachers! (Glaap, 1984, pp.88-90).

Consequently, when Russell left school at 15 he only had one O-level, in English, and the vague idea of becoming a writer. However, with his social background he had no idea how to go about it. So he worked as a ladies' hairdresser until he was 20. Although he regarded art as alien to his world, he did become interested in the Liverpool Beat Poets (among them the Roger McGough mentioned by Rita in Act 1, scene 1) and in folk-music. He played the guitar in pubs and wrote some songs.

Russell describes his initial distaste for plays and the theatre as follows, 'Theatre had always seemed to me a highbrow slap in the face to people like me. I just couldn't relate to it, either culturally or socially; it didn't seem to me to be about people like me, and people like me never seemed to go and look at it.' (*The Independent*, 23.1.88). In another interview he expanded on this view:

> They are bourgeois plays because they are written by the bourgeoisie for the bourgeoisie ... you have a generation of working-class people who have never known the habit of going to the theatre, who have been totally intimidated, who would never dare to presume to go to these places ... in the twenties – and thirties and forties – you still had this middle-class strangle-hold on the theatre, excluding whole sections of our society. (Jones, pp.21-22)

His ideas changed dramatically when his girlfriend, now his wife, took him to Liverpool's Everyman Theatre. The experience is echoed by Rita's enthusiasm for her first visit to the theatre. At that time, in the early seventies, regional drama was being encouraged by a group of young directors in some major northern English cities. Russell commented, 'They turned it into a real local people's theatre ... The working class voice was allowed to be heard.' (*The Independent*, 23. 1. 88). This experience showed him what kind of things he wanted to write and made him decide to study drama at a teacher's training college. But first, at the age of twenty, he had to start taking O-level and A-level exams and raise the money to pay for his studies. His reasons for returning to full-time education were similar to Rita's – he 'wanted to know everything', to catch up on all the culture he had missed. And so he recommenced his education at St Katharine's College of Education. When he left in 1973 he started work as a teacher, but the success of his play *John, Paul, George, Ringo and Bert* in 1974, about Russell's experiences as a 14-year-old Beatles fan, enabled him to give up teaching and become a full-time writer.

During his studies Russell had decided that he wanted to write for working class audiences. Indeed, he is remarkable because no other British playwright has ever had such a series of successes all dealing with the lives of the working-class. He is one of a group of left-wing Merseyside writers which has recently emerged and which has been immensely popular in the theatre, television and film. Almost every theatre in Britain has staged *Educating Rita*. It was written in 1979 and first performed a year later in London. In 1983 it was made into a film with the close collaboration of Russell himself.

Educating Rita is a passionate plea for everyone's right to a decent education. Russell feels strongly that the working class is being denied access to many aspects of the national culture. Their limited access to cultural products is partly due to expectations about their tastes and abilities. But it is also partly a result of their own attitudes. Russell differs from many other writers on 'working class culture' in that he does not romanticise about it, but exposes bigotry and resistance to change. Rita illustrates a theme found in many of his major plays since the mid-1970s: someone driven by a sense of frustration fights for an education that will help them to break through the limitations of the class and culture into which they were born.

Educating Rita also expresses Russell's resentment towards those who believe that art is only for a highly educated minority. He attacks the elitism of what he describes as the 'literature industry', consisting of an opera industry, a theatre industry and many who work in these fields, such as producers, directors, the editors of theatre magazines and critics:

There's something I call the 'literature industry' which has sprung up and which I particularly loathe because it seems to me to put a huge barrier between the Ritas of this world who want to learn and literature itself. It probably comes out in my own sort of situation; for years and years and years I wouldn't pick a classical or known and regarded author from the book-shelves. I'd rather read a racy, accessible American novel or indeed quality American novels because they were rarely classified as literature ... (I'm) trying to attack the divisions really in teaching, in education, and in the class system. And so it's the division and it's the elitist way in which literature is dealt with that I really object to. (Glaap, 1984, p.21-22)

Russell describes his aim in writing *Educating Rita* as follows, 'I wanted to make a play which engaged and was relevant to those who had no knowledge of literature, those who considered themselves uneducated, those whose daily language is not the language of the university or the theatre.' (Glaap, 1984, p.5). A comment in *The Independent* newspaper (23.1.88) verifies that Russell's plays 'are still aimed ... at the kind of people whose hair he cut'. Interestingly, despite his fame, Russell has remained in Liverpool, refusing to move to London partly out of fear that he would be sucked into the middle classes.

SOME OF RUSSELL'S MOST IMPORTANT PLAYS

John, Paul, George, Ringo and Bert	1974
Breezeblock Park	1975
Our Day Out	1977
Educating Rita (stage)	1980
Blood Brothers	1983
Educating Rita (film)	1983
Shirley Valentine	1986

The Plot

Dr. Frank Bryant, a university lecturer in his early fifties, needs some extra money to pay for his drinking habit, so he agrees to tutor an Open University student. He is confronted with Rita, a brash twenty-six-year-old Liverpudlian hairdresser. Although she is very intelligent, she did not get much of an education at school, largely because in the working class area where she was brought up school achievment was regarded as an attempt to be better than everyone else. Yet despite her poor education she has a mind of her own and expresses her opinions honestly and spontaneously.

Rita has always felt that there was more to life than the everyday routine. She realises that her poor education stands in the way of a better quality life. Eventually she becomes so unhappy that she decides to acquire that education. She explains to Frank that she wants to find out what she has missed. She wants, for instance, to be able to make more informed choices about art and literature instead of simply rejecting 'highbrow' culture automatically because it is not part of traditional working class life. In fact, she wants nothing less than a whole education, 'a better culture'.

Rita finds her working class environment narrow and confining. She suffers from a lack of mental stimulation and is frustrated with the inflexible attitudes of those around her. No one understands why she cannot settle for the traditional role of wife and mother. She suspects that people feel threatened by her desire for change, as if she were rejecting their life styles and values. Signing on for the Open University course was a difficult decision because she knew that education would change her and may even alienate her from her present environment. But her desire for change is so strong that she is prepared to take the risk.

Rita is alert, observant and eager to learn. She loves literature, and has even changed her name from Susan to Rita in admiration of a novel by Rita Mae Brown, *Rubyfruit Jungle*. But her approach is naive and she cannot discriminate between writers of acknowledged good quality and popular fiction. Frank finds her enthusiasm refreshing, but sees that her reactions are highly subjective and that she is completely ignorant of the accepted code of literary criticism. He realises that in order to pass exams she will have to suppress her spontaneous, emotional response to literature. He is aware of the danger that she might become like his other students, who give him the conventional, second-hand opinions of literary critics rather than their own feelings. Because he does not want Rita to lose her originality Frank tries to dissuade her from taking the course. But she insists.

Rita's home life gradually becomes more and more difficult. She had enrolled for the course against her husband, Denny's, wishes. He takes a traditional view of the role of women and wants her to stop taking the pill and have a child. He cannot understand her need for better choices in life. He himself is content if he is offered eight different kinds of beer. As Rita describes the situation at home to Frank she attacks the system which denies working class people meaningful choices of what to do with their lives.

Frank precipitates a crisis when he invites Rita and Denny to a dinner party. Denny refuses, but Rita sets out alone. Standing outside Frank's house she looks in through the window and realises that she cannot go in. She has become a cultural misfit, alienated from her working class environment, but not belonging to Frank's world either. Sadly, she joins her family in the pub. She has already decided to give her studies up when her mother starts crying and makes a remark which shows how disappointed she is with her own life. This changes Rita's mind. She becomes even more determined not to become trapped like her mother.

When Denny finds out that Rita is still taking the pill, against his wishes, he burns her books and gives her the ultimatum of either giving the course up or leaving home. But by now Rita's studies have become so important to her that they represent life itself. She can no more give them up than she can stop breathing. So she moves out.

Half way through the play Rita attends a summer school in London and comes back a changed person, outwardly and inwardly. She has become much more self-confident and has learned a lot about her subject. To Frank's dismay she has already read the poems of William Blake. Her reactions to them prove Frank's worst fears. She has learned to discuss literature in controlled, analytic terms and her spontaneous, passionate reactions to it have been suppressed. Rita has now found the 'better culture' she was seeking. She copies the life styles and opinions of educated people around her, such as her flatmate, Trish. But as Rita becomes more knowledgeable, Frank falls into an even deeper depression. For a while she had given his teaching some meaning, a sense of purpose. He had come to depend on her visits. But now the old Rita has practically disappeared and the new one no longer needs him. There are whole areas of her life about which he knows nothing. She had not told him, for instance, about her new flatmate or about her change of job. He is so disappointed that he even tells her he will be glad to see her leave. Gradually, their positions are reversed: Rita turns into an academic, skillfully applying the analytic methods of literary criticism which Frank has taught her, whilst he himself longs for emotional responses to the literature he loves.

After summer school the relationship between Frank and Rita changes dramatically. More and more, we feel that they are exchanging places. For whereas Rita is asserting her independence from her tutor, he is growing increasingly dependent on her. At one time Frank was Rita's only hope, but now she seems to be the only person he can relate to. But their old familiarity has gone. He is no longer the focal point of her life. She is forming other relationships and hardly shows any personal interest in him at all any more. Besides, she is now more interested in art and literature than in other people. As she becomes an 'expert' on literature, the originality and honesty which once distinguished her from the average student are buried by conventional, second-hand opinions.

The depths of Frank's despair are revealed when he turns up drunk for a lecture and makes some bitter, ironic comments on the literary establishment, including himself as part of it. Rita's development has made him even more aware of how destructive traditional methods of teaching literature can be. Eventually his new preference for subjective, emotional responses, together with his drinking, lead to his taking a forced sabbatical.

Things come to a head between Frank and Rita when he asks for her opinion on some of his poems. Instead of giving him her honest, personal reactions, she repeats the complicated, pretentious interpretation of her flatmate. Frank is bitterly disappointed. During the ensuing quarrel he suggests that Rita's new-found 'culture' is superficial and that all she is doing is imitating others. She accuses him, and the middle classes altogether, of preferring the working class to remain uneducated so that they can be patronised. After this all contact between Rita and her tutor seems to stop until Frank tries to ring her about her exam. This is when he finds out something else she had not told him, that she has reverted to her original name of Susan.

After the exam, Frank is packing for Australia when Rita returns to thank him. Finally she has realised that he was right. She had been so hungry for education and culture that she had accepted the life styles and opinions of educated people unquestioningly. Now she realises that Frank had been warning her not to be taken in by appearances and to try to retain her honesty and spontaneity. She has also been affected by the attempted suicide of her flatmate, Trish, on whom she had modelled herself. Under Trish's veneer of culture her life had really been empty and meaningless. Rita understands now that to lead a more meaningful life she must do more than talk about literature and copy educated people.

Frank recognises the old Rita and asks her to accompany him to Australia. But Rita has only just begun to take control of her own life and does not want to be pressed into making any decisions yet. There are several alternatives, but it does not seem to matter which one she chooses. With her new confidence and skills, she has achieved her aim of acquiring a better quality of personal choices. She has also managed to balance the old Rita, the hairdresser, with Susan, the educated woman. After a period of simply exchanging one set of conventions for another, she has now rediscovered her independence of mind. For her, education has been a liberating experience, after all.

Act 1, Scene 1
Rita goes to see her Open University tutor, Dr Frank Bryant. She explains what she wants from the course. Frank is reluctant to teach her.

Act 1, Scene 2
Rita needs to change her subjective approach to literature. She tells Frank about her school days.

Act 1, Scene 3
Rita has to become more discriminating in her reading.

Act 1, Scene 4
Denny does not like Rita's studying. Rita explains her views on 'working class culture'. She finally understands the meaning of Forster's phrase 'only connect'.

Act 1, Scene 5
Denny burns Rita's books. Frank explains why he stopped writing poetry. Rita persuades Frank to go with her to see her first play.

Act 1, Scene 6
Rita is so overwhelmed by *Macbeth* that she has to tell Frank about it. Frank invites Rita and Denny to a dinner party.

Act 1, Scene 7
Rita did not turn up at Frank's dinner party. She feels like a social misfit. Her mother's regret makes her determined to go on with her education.

Act 1, Scene 8
Denny has thrown Rita out. Her essay on *Macbeth* is still too emotional. Frank is unwilling to change her way of thinking, but she insists.

Act 2, Scene 1

After summer school Rita is more self-confident. She no longer informs Frank about changes in her life, such as her new flatmate. She even tries to influence him. He realises that she is losing her originality. Frank and Rita seem to be exchanging places: Frank is looking for a direct, emotional reaction to literature, while she discusses it in a more detached manner.

Act 2, Scene 2

Rita is very much influenced by Trish. She feels that at last she has found 'a better culture'. Frank is afraid that she will regard the opinions of literary authorities as absolute truths. Now she is writing the same kind of essay as his other students.

Act 2, Scene 3

Frank has been reported for drunkenness. He criticises Rita's work for being full of borrowed ideas, but admits that it would get a good mark in an exam. She feels she no longer needs his guidance.

Act 2, Scene 4

Rita has not told Frank about her change of job. She prefers to talk about more interesting things with people who are 'not trapped'. They quarrel and Frank suggests that she can no longer see what really matters in life. He asks for her opinion on some of his poems.

Act 2, Scene 5

Frank is bitterly disappointed with Rita's second-hand judgements of his poems. Sarcastically, he suggests that he has created a monster. Rita accuses him of taking his education for granted.

Act 2, Scene 6

Frank and Rita now have so little contact that he has to ring her at work to give her the details of her exam. He does not know, either, that she has reverted to her original name of Susan.

Act 2, Scene 7

Frank has been advised to take a two year sabbatical. He is packing for Australia when Rita comes back to thank him and tell him that he was right. She had mistaken the veneer of culture for real education. Trish's attempted suicide also showed her that there is more to life than art and literature. For the first time in her life, she has real, meaningful choices.

Summary of the Play

ACT 1, SCENE 1

The play opens with Dr Frank Bryant in his study at the university where he is Senior Lecturer in English. He is searching among the books on his shelves. Then he finds what he was looking for, a bottle of whisky hidden behind one of the books. He has just taken his first drink when the phone rings. From the conversation we gather that he is speaking to a woman, probably his wife or girlfriend. It becomes clear that their relationship is not very harmonious, probably because she does not like his drinking. We also learn that Frank is waiting for an Open University student. From the phone conversation we conclude that Frank is witty, with a taste for irony.

The phone call is interrupted by someone knocking at the door. Although he repeatedly invites his visitor to come in, the knocking continues. Eventually his new student, Rita, bursts into the room. She is annoyed and reproaches Frank about the door handle, which needs mending. Frank is taken aback by this unconventional entrance. When he asks Rita for her name she does not understand his question 'You are ...?' She is obviously not used to formal situations. From Rita's first appearance we conclude that she is a very open, direct sort of person.

As the scene progresses Rita explains why she wants to take the Open University course. For a long time she has been feeling 'out of step' with everyone around her, as if she were dancing to a different tune. At twenty-six everyone is surprised that she has not yet had a baby. She has lied to her husband, telling him that she is no longer taking the pill, but she herself does not want a child yet. First she feels the need to 'discover' herself. Neither her husband nor her neighbours and friends would be able to understand this. When she tries to explain to her husband that she wants a change, all he can suggest is moving house. Rita feels starved of intellectual stimulation and has decided to try to discover and develop the potential which she feels is inside her. She is aware that this process will involve very deep changes, not the superficial ones which she sees every day at the hairdresser's where she works. She criticises her customers for thinking that changing their hairstyles will somehow transform them into new individuals. Yet, although she says she sometimes hates these women, she also understands that their limited horizons are a result of their poor education. Like these women, Rita has already begun to change in a very superficial way. She was so impressed by a novel written by Rita Mae Brown that she decided to call herself Rita, instead of Susan (White). She knows, though, that real growth must come from within and involve the whole personality.

At present Rita feels imprisoned by the fixed habits and attitudes of the working class people around her. They cling on to what they know and automatically reject anything new, without even trying to understand it. For instance they reject 'highbrow' art forms, such as ballet and opera, labelling them as 'posh' and 'middle class'. Rita finds this kind of intolerance limiting. She imagines that a better education will liberate her from such conventional attitudes and enable her to form her own judgements. But first she needs to find out more about 'highbrow' culture. A course in literature seems to be a good starting point. She envies Frank's ability to make conscious choices about which books to read and which TV programmes to watch and longingly asks him what it is like to be free. Russell himself answered the question of what the Open University course means to Rita in an interview, 'She does want to be able to sit down and discuss books and art and music and to be spiritually fed and, to stay in the metaphor, she feels that she's starving in her present social stratum, that it's arid and that if she moves in this other stratum it will be some sort of oasis' (Glaap, 1984, p.95).

Rita's remarks on culture suggest that the working class tend to prefer 'lowbrow' or 'popular' entertainment which is relatively easy to understand, whereas educated middle class people like Frank prefer something more 'highbrow'. In comparison with Frank, Rita is much more aware of the link between social class, education and cultural tastes. She herself reads indiscriminately and is unaware of any difference between good quality literature and popular pulp fiction. Several humorous misunderstandings arise because of the different levels of knowledge and education. Rita, for instance, thinks that when Frank mentions Yeats, the poet, he is referring to Yates, the wine shop, which is pronounced in the same way. And when she talks about Elliot, she means a Chicago policeman and not the famous poet, T.S.Eliot.

These misunderstandings show Rita how much she needs to learn about literature if she wants to take the Open University exams. She is still a little unsure about taking the course, although she is deadly serious about wanting to learn. She explains that despite her brash manner she really lacks self-confidence. The only thing which prevents her from giving the whole thing up and going home is Frank's personality. She had obviously been expecting a different type of person and admits that she used bad language in order to 'test' him. But because he did not object to her swearing she feels accepted. He does not seem to want to force his own standards on her. Rita finally decides to stay because she likes her tutor. Having made such a difficult decision, her disappointment is acute when Frank suddenly announces that he is no longer willing to teach her. He had only taken the OU course on because of the extra money. Meeting Rita confirms his suspicion that he has made a mistake. He explains that he is not a good teacher, but that this does not matter to the majority of his students. He sees, however, that Rita is different because she expects so much more – she wants to learn 'everything'. Her total ignorance about literary analysis means that he will have to explain things he would normally take for granted. He knows that her thirst for knowledge and also her honesty will not allow her to accept anything she does not understand. This is demonstrated when Rita asks him what 'assonance' means, a word she had picked up from some students on the way to his room. He has obviously never really thought about it and the example he gives is, to her, 'getting the rhyme wrong'. Frank is amused and disarmed by her simple, honest response. He finds her a refreshing change from his other students. Unlike them, she has a genuine love of literature and responds to it directly and spontaneously. Her total ignorance of literary traditions and analysis prevents her from repeating second-hand ideas. It is apparently a long time since he has had such an enthusiastic student. It also seems a long time since he has felt any sense of purpose or fulfilment in his teaching.

Surprisingly, Frank does not immediately grasp this rare opportunity to share his love of his subject and develop Rita's mind. Instead, he refuses to teach her. Knowing how much the course means to her he feels he is not capable of fulfilling her expectations. Also, he probably shies away from so much responsibility. But

Rita refuses to be turned away, insisting that he has agreed to teach her and this is what he must do. As she walks out we are uncertain as to whether she will really come back and, if she does, whether Frank will accept her or not.

This first meeting makes it clear that Rita is not a typical university student. Despite her poor education she has a very independent mind. Her approach to literature is fresh because she has not yet been taught to repeat second-hand opinions about it in order to pass exams. She expresses her opinions honestly and spontaneously. Despite the huge differences between Rita and Frank, they also have something in common, for they are both unhappy and frustrated with their lives and the cultures they belong to. Paradoxically, both try to escape to each other's worlds. Rita sees in Frank the key to a better, freer life and aspires to become 'cultured', like him. However, Frank despises his way of life and finds his middle class, academic environment shallow and pretentious. Rita's unspoiled mind shows him all the more clearly how fragile his own assumptions are. To him she is the first breath of fresh air which has been in his room for years. We sense that he would like to revert to some stage before his literary education began, when his reactions to literature were still like Rita's, unspoiled by received literary opinions.

ACT 1, SCENE 2

Frank is in his study, obviously expecting someone, when he sees the door handle being turned. Since no one enters, he pulls the door open. To his surprise Rita is standing outside, oiling the handle. It seems that their conflict has been resolved. Either they have been in touch with each other or Frank has gradually got used to the idea of teaching her, for the question is no longer discussed. As Rita looks out of the window at the students on the lawns she wistfully tells Frank that as a child she always wanted to go to a public school. From Frank's horrified response we gather that he dislikes the elitism of these institutions. Asked why she did not go on to university after school, Rita explains that in the working class area where she lived nobody expected her to learn. Taking school seriously would have meant being different from her friends and this was 'not allowed'. She would have been an outsider. And so, like the other girls, she concentrated instead on music, clothes and boys and finally got married. But she always felt that there was something missing in her life, until one day she admitted to herself that she was extremely unhappy. This was the point where she had to decide whether to go on pretending and compensate for her unhappiness with new dresses or whether to try to make a new start. The decision was very hard because it meant that she would have to change. She knew that no one would understand her and that she would become alienated from her environment.

Abruptly Rita stops talking and turns to the essay which she has written for Frank on *Rubyfruit Jungle*. (This novel, which Rita admired so much that she changed her name to Rita, after the author Rita Mae Brown, is about an independent-minded, culture-hungry woman called Molly Bolt, a woman, in fact, just like Rita herself). This is where Rita's first lesson in literary criticism begins. Instead of analysing the novel in an objective way she has simply described it and given her personal reactions. Her opinion of E.M.Forster's novel *Howards End* is similarly subjective – 'crap'. She rejects it because the author took no account of the conditions of the poor at the time of writing. Frank is astounded at so much subjectivity and that Rita judges works of art on whether they relate to real life or not. He explains that the orthodox way of writing literary appreciation is to be objective and to support opinions with references to accepted authorities.

However, Rita's undisciplined mind is finding it difficult to concentrate. Suddenly she starts asking Frank personal questions. He is exasperated, but Rita has a great natural curiosity about people and cannot be put off. To satisfy her, Frank tells her he has split up from his wife and is now living with a former student, Julia. His remarks about both women are bitterly sarcastic. We also learn that Frank has a low opinion of himself and finds himself shallow. Nevertheless, Rita envies his 'educated' way of expressing himself. Her naiveté astonishes Frank and again he realises how much he will have to teach her.

Rita is disappointed when he tries to turn the conversation back to *Howards End*. She is reminded of her school days, when teachers often killed off interesting subjects by over-analysing them. Frank's remark that this is what education does earns him a rebuke. Education is so valuable to Rita that she cannot see how anyone could possibly criticise it. She challenges him to explain why he is giving her an education if he is so unsure of its value. Frank's answer is less than convincing, 'Because it's what you want'. His comment that he would actually prefer to take her by the hand and run out of the room forever is partly an attempt to lighten the tone of the conversation, but also partly serious. Rita has let some light and air into his boring, routine existence and it is understandable that he really would like to escape from it all with her.

Rita cannot see that Frank is not merely paying her compliments. She is blind to the cry of despair behind his question 'why didn't you walk in here twenty years ago?' Someone like her could have saved him. He might still be writing poetry, might even have achieved greatness instead of doing a job which was becoming more and more meaningless. Eventually Frank realises that Rita needs him to teach her – him and no one else. In a tone half determined, half angry, he warns her that she will have to work hard and that if she is not prepared to do this she might as well give up already. But Rita has no intention of giving up, nor is she cowed. Once more, she completely disarms him, remarking how impressive he looks when he is angry.

It is highly significant that Rita has to study E. M. Forster's *Howards End* (1910). Like her, the hero, Leonard Bast, comes from the working class and is trying to educate himself, although he lives in poverty. He, too, realises that there is more to life than day to day existence. He loves literature and music, but is living with a woman who cannot understand him. By chance, Leonard gets to know a wealthy, cultured family. At first he denies his humble origins and tries to copy the culture of the upper class, but eventually he progresses beyond mere imitation.

ACT 1, SCENE 3

Rita is working on E.M. Forster's novel *Howards End*, but is having great difficulty understanding it, especially his now famous phrase 'only connect'. Frank cannot accept her essay on it because of all the references to popular fiction. Rita feels this is unfair because, after all, he had told her to refer to other authors. But Frank had forgotten Rita's inability to distinguish between 'good quality' literature and pulp fiction. He had taken it for granted that she would only refer to accepted literary authorities. To Rita all books are 'literature'. When she asks Frank to explain the difference he is confused and embarrassed. It is obvious that he has taken over traditional ideas about what constitutes 'good' literature without really giving the question much thought. Despite his embarrassment, Frank finds Rita refreshing because her reactions to literature have not been shaped by other people. His students and colleagues, on the other hand, are probably no longer able to react to literature in such a direct, honest way because they know what the approved, orthodox reactions should be. From Frank's reaction Rita draws the conclusion that she should stop reading popular fiction. However, he explains that she can go on reading it, as long as she is aware of its position in the literary hierarchy, that it is not usually analysed for its literary qualities, but simply read for enjoyment.

ACT 1, SCENE 4

Rita is still having problems with the phrase, 'only connect', with which Forster introduced his novel *Howards End*. By the end of the scene she has understood it and we see how relevant it is for her own development.

Rita cannot work at home because her husband is against her studying. So to avoid arguments she writes her essays at the hairdressing salon. Of course, if they are busy she does not have much time, which partly accounts for the brevity of her essay on the difficulties of staging Ibsen's play *Peer Gynt*. (Again, Russell's choice of this particular play is significant, since it is about someone who is searching for the meaning of life). In fact, her essay only consisted of the one sentence, 'Do it on the radio'. When Frank confronts her about it her explanation completely disarms him because it shows that she has understood Ibsen's intentions very well. She argues that since he wrote it as a play for voices, he would have solved the staging difficulties by presenting it as a radio play if this medium had existed. Once again,

Frank is impressed by the originality of Rita's thinking. Nevertheless, he realises that he still has a lot of work to do. In order to pass exams she must learn – and be willing to accept – the orthodox method of writing essays on literature.

Scene four is particularly important because of Rita's opinions on working class culture. Russell is certainly using her as a mouthpiece when she denies the existence of a specific working class culture. (See Themes for further details). Her view is that although the working class think they have culture, there is no real meaning to their lives, even though materially speaking they might be quite well off. (Today the situation is different. The old working class has divided into a new working class with a somewhat higher status and an impoverished underclass). Rita describes a vicious circle of frustration and compensation through consumer goods. She feels that the working class is manipulated by the mass media and that their choices in life, although many, are really very narrow – quantity as opposed to quality. This reflects the author's own conviction that the working class is deprived of good quality choices.

As Rita speaks, Frank notes her understanding of the underlying structures of society and asks why she did not study politics instead of literature. Rita, however, hates politics, probably because she feels that politicians are not interested in changing the situation of the working class in any fundamental way. Frank uses Rita's description of the vicious circle of working class life to demonstrate to her that she does indeed understand Forster's phrase 'only connect', but was not aware of how it related to herself. This is an important step in Rita's development because it makes her more conscious of how various phenomena are interrelated. It will help her to think in a more structured way.

Asked why he did not simply tell her what Forster's phrase meant from the beginning, Frank explains that he prefers to allow her to find things out for herself. We begin to suspect that he is a much better teacher than he himself believes.

Frank's suggestion that there is nothing wrong with working class life as long as people are happy shows that he does not know anything about the working class. Furthermore, he is not interested in them. Here Russell is illustrating the barriers which exist between the classes. He is also implying that the better educated do not care about those less privileged than themselves. (For further details see Themes).

ACT 1, SCENE 5

Rita arrives for her tutorial without an essay which she was supposed to write. Denny found out that she was secretly on the pill and was so angry that he burned her books and papers, including the essay. He cannot understand why she does not want a child yet and feels that she is denying him his right to have children. In the previous scene Rita told Frank that Denny had tried to stop her attending her tutorial, wanting her to go out with him and his friends instead. Rita believes he feels threatened because she is trying to break away from the traditional working class way of life. He cannot understand her desire for more meaningful choices in life than materialistic ones such as eight different kinds of beer. She told her husband that she would have a baby if and when she chose to. Rita understands Denny's feelings and is sorry for him. She knows that he is so fixed in his ways and in his thinking that he is incapable of understanding her needs. He must feel that she has in some way betrayed him by changing into a different person.

In view of the seriousness of the situation Frank would prefer to discuss Rita's future. But she explains that she can no more give up her studies than she can give up breathing. The course represents life itself to her, she lives for nothing else. She tells Frank that he gives her 'room to breathe', that he 'feeds her'. At this Frank warns that art and literature should not become more important than real life. Rita, however, insists on going on with the tutorial. She has made the decision to continue her education, even though it may cost her her marriage. More than ever before Frank realises just how much it means to her and what the cost might be. He had never really understood how much she had been up against. And now she needs help which only he can give.

Characteristically, Rita changes the subject and asks Frank why he stopped writing poetry. He explains that instead of writing poetry he spent years trying to create 'literature'. By this he means the sort of work which would be acceptable to literary critics and could be studied and 'appreciated' by students. He further confuses Rita by his comment that people should not believe in literature. Here Russell himself is speaking. The author is highly critical of what he calls the 'literature industry' and of the elitist way in which literature is dealt with. He questions the absolute status of great authors, which is created by this 'literature industry'. (See Themes for more details). Frank's explanation suggests that he drinks in order to suppress his frustration about his teaching, his poetry, the way literature is dealt with by the so-called 'experts' and his personal life.

ACT 1, SCENE 6

Rita bursts into Frank's study, breathless and excited. He is alarmed, imagining that something serious has happened. And it has. Seeing *Macbeth* on stage was a major event in Rita's life. She is still so overwhelmed by the experience that she has to tell someone about it and Frank is the only person she thinks will understand. She had expected Shakespeare to be boring, but had 'wanted to find out'. This is reminiscent of the reason she gave for starting the course in scene 1, 'I wanna know'. She wants to find out what she has missed through not having had a good education.

Frank takes the opportunity to explain what 'tragedy' means in dramatic terms. Rita learns that it is different from the so-called 'tragedies' reported in the type of newspapers she reads. She is surprised that there is so much more to *Macbeth* than just an exciting story. But she is also dismayed because she realises how ignorant she is about literature and the academic code. Her reactions to literature are still limited to a purely emotional response.

Rita's first visit to a 'proper' theatre echoes an important event in the author's own life. When he first started going to the theatre it seemed very far removed from his own working class background. Then, in the early seventies, things changed. A group of young directors in some northern English cities were beginning to encourage new, local playwrights and this marked a turning-point for Russell. He enjoyed this new type of play so much that he started studying drama and decided to write plays especially for working class people like himself.

As Rita is leaving to go back to the hairdressing salon Frank invites her to a dinner party at his house. She is stunned. Why should he invite her? What could she possibly contribute? What does he want of her? Surprised, he simply suggests that she might enjoy it. This was an aspect she had not considered. When Frank extends the invitation to include Denny, Rita has a mental picture of her husband among Frank's guests. She already knows that he will refuse.

ACT 1, SCENE 7

When Rita appears for her next tutorial she is confronted by an angry Frank. She and Denny had not turned up at his dinner party and Rita's only explanation had been a brief note of apology which she had scribbled on the back of her essay and put through his letter box. She explains that Denny had refused to go and they had quarrelled. So she had set off alone. It had been difficult to find the house, but eventually she had arrived outside Frank's door. Through the window she could see him and his guests talking and laughing. Suddenly she realised she could not go in. She had brought the wrong sort of wine and was probably wearing the wrong clothes. But, above all, she was afraid of making a fool of herself. The only way she could join in the conversation would be to amuse them all by her witty remarks. But she did not want to 'play the court jester', as she puts it. She wanted to be taken seriously, to be accepted on their terms. So she had written the note and gone to join her family in the pub.

Frank reproaches Rita for upsetting Julia's arrangements, but we suspect that really he was very disappointed. Because he himself is so fascinated by her he imagines that everyone else will find her equally delightful. He had not stopped to consider the embarrassing position he had put Rita in. This lack of understanding once again shows that he is completely unaware of the difficulties facing people from her background. After suggesting that she should see a psychiatrist he asks why she does not simply give the course up if it is causing so many problems. Why not just stay with her family and join in the singing in the pub? Rita has to explain that it is impossible for her to revert to her former life. She has begun to find out what was missing and can no longer stop. She did try to join in with the singing, but it was no good. She is in a no man's land, trapped between two worlds. Her old life has slipped away, but a new one is not yet in reach.

As Rita sat among her singing relatives in the pub her mother started to cry. When Rita asked what was wrong she explained, 'because we could sing better songs than those'. Denny chose to ignore his mother-in-law's unhappiness and cheered her up again. He prefers a facade of happiness to the truth because facing up to problems usually means making some kind of changes. But Denny does not have the courage for that.

Rita sees that her mother is disappointed and frustrated with the emptiness of her life, but cannot do anything about it. Through the contrasts with her mother and Denny we see even more clearly how difficult it is for Rita to break away, to sing her own song. Rita sees her mother's tears as a warning not to become trapped, too, and becomes even more determined to give her own life as much meaning as she can by creating better choices for herself.

ACT 1, SCENE 8

Rita comes into Frank's study, carrying a suitcase. Denny has issued the ultimatum that she must either give up her studies and stop taking the pill or leave. He feels she is betraying him and his social origins – also her own – by rejecting the traditional working class way of life. He seems to need her to live by the accepted code in order to reinforce and justify his own values. Rita understands him and concedes that from his point of view he is right. But it is more important to her not to betray herself. She feels she must try to live up to her potential.

Rita has arranged to stay with her parents until she finds a flat. But first she needs to see Frank. With her life disintegrating around her he is the only remaining fixed point. She rejects his attempt to comfort her and insists on discussing her essay on *Macbeth*. Now, more than ever, she needs to feel that some part of her life is solid and valuable.

Frank is bewildered. He would like to comfort and help her, but she will only accept what he can give her as a teacher. What should he say? Her essay is powerful and moving, but far too emotional for exam purposes. To pass exams she would have to change, he would have to change her. And he is not at all sure that he wants to do that because he would risk suppressing her honesty and spontaneity. He might completely destroy her uniqueness. Her independent mind might become full of second-hand opinions and literary jargon.

Rita cannot see Frank's problem at all. After all, she *wants* to change. That was the whole point of taking the course. She begins to wonder if he is trying to tell her gently that she is not good enough. When he reassures her about that she comes to another conclusion, that he probably finds it too difficult to teach someone like her, with her untutored mind and her background. She explains that criticism will not hurt her feelings. On the contrary, she needs him to set clear standards, otherwise she cannot realise her ambition of writing essays and passing exams like all his other students.

By the end of Act 1 the play has reached a climax. Rita's marriage has broken up and she has become alienated from her original environment. Now she can only go forward. To make it all worthwhile she must fulfil her ambition of joining the ranks of the educated, learning their codes, speaking their language, knowing which kind of wine to buy. First she has to come up to the same standard as the other students, which she must prove by passing the same exams. We wonder whether she will manage all this without, as Frank fears, losing too much of her uniqueness.

ACT 2, SCENE 1

As part of her Open University course Rita has attended a summer school in London. She bursts into Frank's study to tell him about it. Outwardly, she has altered her style of dressing and Frank soon realises that she has also changed in other, less superficial ways. London itself offered many new experiences and on the course she met new people and learned more about her subject. She has obviously become more self-confident about expressing her views on literature and is particularly proud of the first time she asked a question in front of a lecture-room full of people.

After relating her experiences she enquires about Frank's holiday in France. From his brief, hesitant remarks we conclude that it was not too successful. Then he explains that Julia left him, although she has since returned. Frank gathers from Rita's conversation that she has a new friend, Trish. Although he does not say anything he must feel hurt that Rita no longer tells him everything. Rita obviously admires Trish for her culture and good taste. She embodies everything Rita ever wanted. She tells Frank how much she is enjoying her present life and how she feels young and alive again among her fellow-students.

When Rita gives Frank a present of a pen solely for writing poetry his thanks are rather subdued, probably because he resents this attempt to influence him. Rita then suggests that they discuss next term's work outside on the grass, but Frank refuses. So she tries to let

some air in through the window. We are reminded of
their first meeting, when Frank saw her as the first
breath of fresh air that had been in his stuffy, academic
room for years. But now, significantly, the window will
not open. The refreshing, irreverent Rita of the beginning has disappeared and the new one cannot let any
fresh air in. She is gradually turning into a 'normal'
student, just like all the others.

As Frank takes his whisky bottle from its hiding place
Rita reproaches him for drinking so much. This is new,
too. She never used to try to change him, but accepted
him as he was. He wonders what would happen if he
agreed to reform, to please her, and then she left. Where
would he be then? Rita is taken aback. She lives so
much in the present that she has not thought about the
time after her exams. She is shocked when Frank says
that not only is her going inevitable, but that he will
actually be pleased when she leaves. He sees that she is
hurt by his comment and does not have the heart to
explain. So he reassures her by lightly brushing it aside.
But he was serious. He knows that as she becomes an
'expert' on literature he will dislike her more and more.
But he also knows that she would not understand his
fears and that, in any case, he can no longer stop her
from becoming a 'proper' student, with all that this
entails.

Instead, he tells her about a poet he had been saving
up for her. He obviously loves William Blake and is
looking forward to Rita's reactions. He expects her to
see the poems as he does, without over-complicating
them. Rita astonishes him by reciting one of Blake's
poems from memory. She 'did' him at summer school.
Frank feels as if he has been robbed of his most
precious possession. He had been saving this gift up,
looking forward to the time when he could help her to
understand him properly, in the way that most literary

critics did not. And now his gift is not appreciated. Rita is not aware of his dismay as she proves to him how much she knows about Blake. As he listens, Frank realises that to her Blake is just another poet, to be ticked off as part of a course on English literature. She had been introduced to him before she was ready and by someone who knew nothing about her and was not concerned about her progress. She should not have read Blake without him.

The incident about Blake suggests that Frank and Rita are gradually beginning to exchange places. Whilst Rita discusses the poems in the sophisticated manner of a student of literature, Frank's reaction is a more direct, emotional one, rather like Rita's approach to literature when they first met.

It is interesting that Russell chose William Blake's two sets of poems, *Songs of Innocence and Experience* for Rita to study at summer school. The first set, *Songs of Innocence*, begun in 1789, is about childlike innocence and ideals, whereas the *Songs of Experience* are often bitter as they describe how these ideals turn into illusions. The poem which Rita recites, *The Sick Rose*, is one of the *Songs of Experience*. Russell's choice of Blake's collection symbolises Rita's progress from innocence to experience as she learns more about literature and literary criticism. But it can also be seen as a warning that her dreams may turn sour.

ACT 2, SCENE 2

Rita is late for her class. When she finally arrives she speaks in an unnatural, upper-middle class voice. Apparently Trish finds Rita's way of speaking ugly and is trying to persuade her to talk 'properly'. Frank does not seem too pleased that Rita has found another mentor. Again and again he notices how she tries to imitate her new flatmate. In fact, Trish has opened up a whole new way of life to Rita. At long last she has been admitted to a world of books, plants and the 'right' furniture, a world in which people know which wines to buy. Finally she has acquired 'a better culture'. Rita's mention of plants is significant because it echoes something in Russell's own life. In an interview he once described his family background:

> I came from a house in which we wouldn't have a plant, we wouldn't have a picture, we wouldn't sit at a table, we'd have food on our knees whilst watching telly. So when I first moved into a different world, before I went to college, and started to mix with people, I'd go into people's houses and they'd have all these things – they didn't live their lives for things, it was just a natural expression of their sensibilities on the whole. One used to want not the pictures, not the plants but what one saw as the ritual way of living. A calmer, more fulfilling life. It's only later on that you find out that is just a particular veneer and that life can be just as arid, if you think it will be better if you have the right pictures on the wall and the right plants. (Jones 1989, p.334)

This description makes it clear that *Educating Rita* is partly a description of Russell's own attempt to acquire a 'better culture'.

Rita's excuse for being late was that she had been unavoidably delayed, but a few minutes later she says she actually arrived early and was talking to some students. Frank notes that her tutorials used to be far too important for her to arrive late, but says nothing. He only expresses surprise that she had the courage to address other, 'proper' students. The fact that she no longer stands in awe of them shows how much she has gained in both knowledge and self-confidence. She even boasts to Frank about how she corrected one of the students.

Frank realises just how much she has changed. She has indeed learned to recognise what is normally classed as 'good' literature – he had taught her himself – but now she proclaims her judgements as absolute truths. How can he explain to her that people still have the right to their own preferences? She does not notice the sarcasm in his comment, 'So you finished him off, did you, Rita?'.

Rita tells Frank that one of the students, Tyson, nicknamed Tiger, has invited her to go to France with a whole group. Frank immediately protests that she cannot go. But he knows that the reason which he gives, her exams, is not the real one. He is jealous and afraid of losing her. Up to now he had been the focal point in her life and had not realised that she would begin to form new relationships. He sees that his influence over her is dwindling. There are whole areas of her life about which he knows nothing. She is becoming a stranger, slipping away from him. Soon she will leave and take all the meaning in his life with her.

When Rita mentions Tiger a second time Frank loses his patience. But Rita's reaction clearly signals that he has gone too far. She is shocked by his suggestion that she is in love with Tiger. Abruptly she breaks off the conversation and asks for his opinion on an essay she has written. When he tells her it would not look out of place with a pile of work done by other, 'proper' students she is delighted. Finally she has made it. She is just as well educated as all the others. She does not notice the irony of Frank's remark. The originality and honest responses to literature which once distinguished her from his other students have been buried by conventional, second-hand opinions and so now her essay is no different from all the others.

ACT 2, SCENE 3

Frank has disgraced himself by turning up drunk for one of his lectures. Back in his study he tells Rita what happened. He was apparently so out of control that he fell off the rostrum and now some students have reported him. As he relates the incident we begin to feel that he has sunk to a new level of despair. Perhaps it was the realisation that the old Rita has finally disappeared which made him give up any pretence of taking his teaching seriously. During the lecture he mentioned Rita's definition of assonance, 'getting the rhyme wrong'. But this dated back to the time when her opinions were all her own. Today she would ridicule her former ignorance and quote a more sophisticated, scholarly definition.

Frank's comment about assonance was a bitter attack on the literary establishment, which takes itself so seriously but, he feels, fails to help people appreciate literature properly. His bitterness is also directed against himself, for he is part of this establishment. The process of educating Rita has shown him even more clearly than before how empty and destructive traditional methods of teaching literature can be.

As soon as Rita sees the state Frank is in she suggests postponing the tutorial. But he insists on discussing an essay she has written on one of Blake's poems. He had expected her to react to it emotionally, without over-complicating it with literary analysis. Instead, she has interpreted it in a very academic way and has obviously taken over other people's opinions, especially those of Trish and some fellow students. When she defiantly asks if her essay is wrong Frank is forced to admit that it would get a good mark in an exam. Its trendiness and sophistication would make it acceptable to most of his colleagues. What he dislikes about it is that her interpretation is second-hand. Once, he thought regretfully, she would have seen the poem for what it is, a simple piece about a flower, described from a child's point of view. The new Rita dissected it with a clinical, analytic eye, searching for symbolism and hidden meaning.

Rita, however, rejects Frank's criticism. She suspects that his pride is hurt because she has not echoed his own ideas. She also accuses him of being unfair because he is criticising the very thing he always wanted her to do, namely to be objective and consult recognised authorities. Ruefully, Frank has to admit that she has a point. He sees how impossible it is to explain his dilemma to her – how to balance the teaching of traditional literary studies with encouraging a true love of literature and honest, personal responses to it. He can only warn her to be careful.

Rita does not understand Frank's warning. He means that whilst consulting the experts she should not let her own reactions be submerged. But she will not allow him to spoil her new-found knowledge, knowledge which has been so hard to acquire. She asserts her independence, accusing him of being over-possessive and telling him she no longer needs his guidance. We begin to wonder whether she even sees herself as his equal. Indeed, there are several signs that their roles are being reversed. Now, for instance, it is Frank rather than Rita who swears. He also takes over her expression 'off my cake'. Russell seems to be suggesting that they are gradually changing places when Frank sits her down in his own chair. Their reactions to Blake's poem also show that Frank prefers a simple, emotional response, whereas Rita discusses it in the analytic way characteristic of teachers of literature. The idea of role reversal is supported by Frank's enjoyment of the very book, *Rubyfruit Jungle*, which once impressed Rita so much that she changed her name. Condescendingly, she informs him that although it is quite interesting it could never be described as quality literature.

ACT 2, SCENE 4

Rita is late for a tutorial. Her suggestion that they should cancel the session altogether suggests that her lessons are no longer important to her. When she was so late Frank rang the hairdresser's, but was informed that she had not worked there for quite a while. He is hurt and reminds her that she always used to tell him everything. Rita is embarrassed, but also annoyed, resenting this intrusion into her private life. She snaps that she does not want to talk about such a 'boring, insignificant detail' as her change of job. One of her reasons for leaving the hairdresser's was that people never talked about anything important, only 'irrelevant rubbish'. Frank remembers the time when he could hardly get Rita to concentrate on her classes because she was so fascinated by the 'boring, insignificant details' of other people's lives – especially his own, he thought ruefully. But apparently the conversation in the bistro where she now works is more interesting. Jealously, Frank asks if Tiger is one of her customers. Rita explains that she enjoys being with the young people in the bistro because they feel strongly about 'things that matter' and are 'not trapped'. Frank does not show how much her comments hurt him. Does she not realise how passionately he feels about the things that matter to him? Yes, he is trapped. He is a poet and does not feel at home in the academic establishment. It is because he is so trapped by his job that he drinks and puts on a cynical, ironic facade. But there is no point in trying to explain all this to Rita. She probably would not be interested.

This was not the first time Rita was late for a tutorial. She has even missed some altogether. Frank suggests that she might want to stop coming. With his back to her, Rita cannot see the expression on his face. She does not know how important the sessions are to him, how he has come to depend on them. Pathetically, like a discarded lover, he complains that she does not seem to be able to stand his company at all any more. Her reply that she has to attend the tutorials because of her exam cuts him deep. He shows his disappointment by his comment, 'I'd rather you spared me that'.

Frank is about to pour himself a drink to ease the pain when Rita rebukes him and adds that it is not worth coming to his tutorials because he has nothing important to say. He responds by querying whether she is still capable of recognising what really matters. We are reminded of his warning when he heard that her marriage was breaking up (Act 1, scene 5), 'When art and literature begin to take the place of life itself, perhaps it's time to ...'. At the time, Rita chose art and literature in preference to real life because she was trying to escape from a deadening environment. But now art and literature really do seem to be more important than her relationships with other people. She does not answer, but reminds him that she is here to discuss literary criticism. He reacts by asking for her opinion on some of his own poetry.

ACT 2, SCENE 5

Frank is sitting in his study, drinking and listening to the radio. We sense his emptiness and desolation. For a short time Rita had given his teaching career a sense of purpose. He had become increasingly dependent on their classes together, feeding on her vivacity, her honesty and her originality. Now that is all gone. After that brief respite, his life has once more become pointless, but this time with no hope of rescue.

To Frank's astonishment, Rita suddenly walks in. She has read his poems together with her flatmate,

Trish. However, Frank is bitterly disappointed when he hears their pompous, pretentious interpretation. Rita was about the only person he thought he could rely on for an honest opinion. His comments are bitterly ironic, but Rita does not notice. Sarcastically, he remarks that he has done a fine job on her and compares himself with Mary Shelley, who wrote *Frankenstein.*

Mary Wollstonecraft Shelley (1797-1851), the wife of the poet Shelley, wrote the novel *Frankenstein* in 1817. It tells the story of how a scientist creates a human being and brings him to life. Lonely and desperate, the creature becomes uncontrollable and the consequences are disastrous. Rita does not understand the implication that Frank, too, has created a monster. By this he means that he has turned her into so much of an expert on literature that she now relies more on borrowed opinions than on her own. This is exactly what Frank had been afraid of. He has made her suppress her emotions and spontaneity.

Finally, Frank asks Rita to go away because he cannot bear her any longer. Misunderstanding him, she is angry. She imagines that he regrets losing his influence over her now that they are on the same level. She accuses Frank and people like him, that is the middle classes, of deliberately keeping the working class down. This reflects Russell's bitter sense of injustice about the fact that the working class are being deprived of a good education and of the chance to participate more fully in cultural life. He feels that they are not being offered the opportunities to make meaningful choices about their lives:

Whilst the working-classes are accused of being philistines, there is a general attempt in this country to withhold culture from them ... Literature is an invention by the middle-classes for their own benefit. The working-classes haven't accepted literacy yet, which is why it is so difficult teaching working-class kids whose traditions are in the spoken word. That's why I write for the theatre, because it's connected with the spoken rather than the written word. (Charles 1983, No. 148. pp.20-21)

Rita tells Frank that she no longer needs him now that she has found a 'better culture'. When she describes it Frank is surprised. Was that really all she wanted, a room full of books, knowing what clothes to wear, what wine to buy, what plays to see and what papers and books to read? To him that seems very little.

Rita cannot understand why Frank despises everything she has ever coveted. For him getting an education and acquiring culture was so much easier. He took it all for granted, whilst she had to make so many sacrifices. His mockery is like a slap in the face. Angrily she accuses him of squandering his opportunities.

Frank is deeply disappointed. He has tried to educate her, to show her what culture is and now he sees that Rita mistakes the mere attributes of culture for culture itself. Whilst acquiring her education she has lost all the qualities which made her a special person, her spontaneity, her originality, her vitality. Frank uses a metaphor to describe the change in her. In the pub her mother had started crying because she felt they could sing better songs. Now he tells Rita that her 'new song' is no better than the old one, but only different and that it sounds shrill, hollow and tuneless. Sadly, he calls her name, wondering if it has all been in vain. But she is blind to his despair and ridicules him for still calling her Rita, the name she rejected as soon as she learned to recognise 'good quality' literature. As she leaves, Frank mockingly asks which author she has decided to imitate next, presumably one of quality, such as Virginia (Woolf), Charlotte (Brontë), her sister Emily or Jane (Austen). He is implying that she will exchange one imitation for another because she can no longer be herself.

ACT 2, SCENE 6

Frank and Rita now have so little contact with each other that he has to ring her at work to give her the details of her exam. He does not know, either, that she has reverted to her original name of Susan.

ACT 2, SCENE 7

Frank's surprise at Rita's entrance shows that he had not expected to see her again. It becomes clear that she no longer knows much about his life. He has narrowly escaped being given the sack for drunkenness at work and is going to spend two years in Australia.

Rita has returned to tell Frank that he is a good teacher and to thank him for entering her for the exam. Then she tells him how, sitting in the exam room, she thought about what he had said and realised he was right. She had been so hungry for education and culture that she had accepted the life style and opinions of educated people without a second thought. She had been dazzled by the trappings of culture – books, trendy, fashionable opinions, easy clichés – and had not wanted any of it to be questioned. Now she knows that Frank had not wanted her to stay ignorant, as she had suspected, but had been warning her to remain honest and retain her ability to distinguish between real and imitation.

Russell once described how he himself went through a similar phase to Rita:

I overvalued to a ludicrous extent the idea of education, what, you know, college and higher education was and went through a period being very much like Rita, you know, being very bored and suffering from 'art in the head'. I used to stop people and ask them what they thought of Chekhov which was very boring for them. Poor souls on the buses." (Glaap 1984, p.95)

Rita has also been affected by Trish's attempted suicide. She had admired her flatmate so much that she had imitated her in everything. The suicide attempt showed her that under Trish's cultured exterior her life was empty and meaningless. Suddenly Rita understands that culture and education do not automatically bring happiness. To lead a fulfilled life she must do more than talk about literature and copy other people's life-styles. Russell seems to be suggesting that she had simply substituted one mediocre existence for another.

With the exam paper lying in front of her, Rita realised that for the first time in her life she had a real, meaningful choice. She could either give a clever, flippant answer and fail or she could answer in the way the examiners expected. She had come back to thank Frank for giving her that choice.

Rita does not know whether the exam will be of any use to her or not. She has not thought about the next step in her life yet, but that is not important. Gradually Frank begins to recognise the old Rita. Hesitantly, he suggests that she could accompany him to Australia. Her reply is evasive. For one thing, Tiger has invited her to go to France with a group of students. But from her comment about him we suspect that she no longer admires him as she used to. Perhaps she finds him superficial, too. Rita now has several choices, but she has only just begun to take control of her own life and does not want to be pressurised into making any decisions. In an interview Russell explained that it does not really matter what she does next:

There's a line in the Paul Simon song *Hearts and Bones*. 'The thought that life could be better is woven indelibly into our hearts and our brains.' It's what my plays are about, the thought that life could be better. I am not interested in how life could be better. I am not interested in whether Rita goes to her mother's, has a baby, finishes her course, or goes to Australia. I am interested that she has got to the point where she can look at those alternatives and feel that she has choice. That for me is the triumph of Rita.' (Jones 1989, p.335)

Frank gives Rita a present which he once bought for 'an educated woman friend'. This reminds us of what Rita said at the beginning (scene 2), that she would not buy a new dress until she had passed her first exam. And then it would be a 'proper' dress, the type worn by educated women. The dress symbolises her graduation as just such an educated woman. As she accepts it Rita regrets that she has only ever taken things from Frank. He protests, but finds it impossible to explain what she has given him, perhaps a sense of purpose and ful-filment. Suddenly it occurs to her that there is one way she can repay him. He is bewildered, not knowing what to expect. Then, in her old role of Rita, the hairdresser, she pulls out her scissors and starts to cut his hair.

The Characters

RITA

Rita White is an outspoken, down-to-earth young woman from Liverpool's working class. She is twenty-six and so far has always played the role expected by her family, friends and neighbours. Although she is intelligent and has a thirst for learning, at school she rejected educational achievement so that she would not become an outsider. Like her classmates, she focussed instead on pop music, clothes and boys. Now and again it occurred to her that she might be missing something, but she allowed herself to be distracted by new clothes, clubs and boys. Consequently, she left school with hardly any qualifications and trained as a hairdresser. Now, at twenty-six, her husband, Denny, is becoming restless because she has not yet had a baby, like all the other young wives in the neighbourhood.

Suddenly Rita rebels against convention. Without her husband's knowledge she continues to take the pill. She somehow feels that life is passing her by and that there is something missing. She is bored by the superficial conversation of her customers and by endless evenings spent in the pub. The lives of those around her seem narrow and confining. Later on in the play she explains that she sees the working class way of life as a disease, a depressing, day-to-day existence, in which people try to compensate for the poor quality of their lives through consumerism. Rita feels, however, that there is no real cure for their frustration because they have been denied the key to a better quality life, namely a good education. Although Rita rejects their limited horizons and inflexible attitudes, she understands and even feels sorry for them. She also sees that it is this lack of education which prevents her husband from envisaging a better quality of choice than eight different kinds of beer in the local pub.

Eventually Rita becomes so unhappy that she resolves to do something about it. She is aware of her intellectual potential and decides to try to 'discover' herself and to find 'a better culture'. She realises that no one around her will understand her attempt to get to know the 'highbrow' kind of culture associated with educated people.

Traditionally the working class reject it as belonging to an alien, elite world, the world of 'them', as opposed to their world of 'us'. Inevitably, her family and friends will feel that she is rejecting them and their norms and values. But Rita is determined to change her life completely. As she herself says, 'if you want to change y' have to do it from the inside'.

Rita's first step in her attempt to catch up on her education and enter a more cultured environment is to enrol for an Open University course in literature. Her first interview with her tutor, Dr Frank Bryant, reveals her total ignorance of literary studies and of the academic way of thinking in general. The only things in her favour are her lively, original mind, her thirst for learning and her passion for reading. She even changed her name from Susan to Rita because she admired a popular novel written by Rita Mae Brown, *Rubyfruit Jungle*. But her hunger for education is not enough to pass exams. At first she is unable to distinguish between literary works of high quality and popular fiction. To her almost every book is 'good' literature. She is also completely ignorant of the methods of literary criticism, thinking that it is sufficient to simply describe her own personal reactions to a book.

Four scenes illustrate Rita's difficulties in learning to appreciate literature from an academic point of view.

The first is Act 1, Scene 2, in which she rejects E.M. Forster's novel *Howards End* because it is not a true reflection of reality. Her tutor is shocked at such a subjective judgement and tells her that first of all she must learn to be more objective and underpin her views with references to accepted authorities. The next lesson follows in Act 1, Scene 3. Acting on Frank's tip that references to other authors impress examiners, Rita has made the mistake of quoting an author of pulp fiction. So now she has to become more selective, which means learning to recognise 'quality' literature. She realises that her mind has not been properly trained, 'My mind's full of junk, isn't it? ... It needs a good clearin' out' (p.32).

Rita's lack of training in exam techniques becomes apparent in Act 1, Scene 4 when she answers an essay topic in one sentence: she would resolve the difficulties of staging Ibsen's *Peer Gynt* by doing it on the radio. Whilst this illustrates the liveliness and originality of her mind, it also shows that she is not aware of the conventional way of answering examination questions. It is significant that when she takes her exam at the end of the play she is asked the very same question. But by then Rita has learned to play by the academic rules and, perhaps more importantly, she makes a conscious choice to apply them.

Another major step in Rita's education is seeing a stage production of *Macbeth* (Act 1, Scene 6). When Frank starts discussing it with her she realises with surprise that academic studies entail more than simply reading or watching works of art. To her the play was no more than an exciting story. She sees that to reach the level of the other, 'proper' students she needs to learn a whole new way of thinking. First of all she must acquire the academic code of analysing and interpreting literature. As her studies progress she learns to discipline her mind and think in a more structural, analytical way.

Frank sets Rita the task of writing an essay on the play which impressed her so much, *Macbeth*. The work she produces presents him with a dilemma. He finds it moving because it is such an honest, passionate description of her experience. The trouble is, it is too emotional for exam purposes. He has to decide whether he really wants to change her approach to literature. If he forces her to treat it in the more distanced, analytic manner of the academic she might lose her ability to react to it spontaneously and honestly. Rita, however, insists on learning how to write the kind of essay which would get a good mark in an exam. Her ambition is to enter the world of educated people, to find 'a better culture' and to do so she must have the passport of a good education. Passing an academic exam becomes a symbol of this better quality life.

Rita's transformation is accompanied by a series of important changes in her personal life. Her marriage breaks up, she moves into a flat with a cultured young woman, gives up her job as a hairdresser to become a waitress in a trendy students' bar and makes new friends among her fellow students. The changes do not come easily. From the outset Rita knew that her quest for a better culture would probably alienate her from her working class background. Although her husband was against her studying she always tried to include him in her new life, inviting him to accompany her to the theatre or, on one occasion, to Frank's house. But he always refused. Gradually, however, the rift between them can no longer be bridged. Rita is aware of Denny's bewilderment as she gradually changes into a different person. In Act 1, Scene 5 she tells Frank that sometimes he gives her presents, hoping that they will bring back the old Susan. She understands his accusation that she has in some way betrayed him by rejecting his way of life. But Rita is growing more aware of her own value as a person and is unwilling to surrender any of her new-found independence.

When Rita embarked on the Open University course she knew that she would probably leave her old life behind. She could not wait for the time when she would be able to move freely among the educated middle classes, accepted as one of them. What she could not foresee was that there would be a period somewhere in between when she would be a cultural misfit, alienated from her old culture, but not yet part of a new one. She becomes aware of this when Frank invites her to a dinner party at his house. Standing outside looking through the window, she suddenly realises that she does not belong to his middle class, academic world. The only way she could make his guests accept her would be to entertain them with comical remarks, but that is beneath her dignity. When she feels lost in a no-man's-land between one culture and another. As she turns away and reluctantly joins her family in the pub she decides to give up her education and with it her hopes of finding a better culture. Then, in the pub, Rita changes her mind abruptly. She is confronted with her mother's own frustration with her life. This makes her all the more determined not to become trapped by the conventions of her class. Her desire to take control over her own life and to improve the quality of her personal choices is reaffirmed.

Gradually, Rita takes her place among the middle class, socialising with her new flatmate and fellow students. A summer school in London marks her entrance into this new culture. For the first time she finds the self-confidence to speak in front of a lecture-room full of people. As she becomes more knowledgeable and self-assured she begins to feel at home with the other students, even to the point of correcting them when they are wrong. She begins to feel that she has outgrown Frank. She no longer needs his guidance and is so fiercely protective of her new independence that she resents him taking any interest in her private life. This is a very different Rita from the young woman who used to constantly interrupt him with personal questions.

As Rita works her way through the great authors she becomes increasingly familiar with the terminology of literary criticism and is soon able to write the same kind of essays as all the other students. She does not understand Frank's warnings that she should not simply take over other people's opinions, merely because they are educated. He notices, for instance, that she is modelling herself on her new flatmate, Trish. And indeed, through Trish Rita has entered into what she feels is 'a better culture'. At last she is moving among educated people, people with the 'right' books and furniture, who know what kind of wine to buy. One day she even imitates Trish's way of speaking. Frank watches in dismay while she becomes a proficient student, but at the same time loses her refreshing honesty and spontaneity. An essay which she wrote on a poem by William Blake, for instance, is full of sophisticated, trendy opinions, but they are all borrowed. She seems to be afraid of expressing her own feelings in case they are not acceptable. Strangely, Rita and Frank appear to be changing places. Whilst she now approaches literature with the objective, analytic eye of the academic, Frank urges her to appreciate it in a more emotional, subjective way.

After Rita comes back from summer school her relationship with Frank begins to deteriorate. First, she starts criticising him, something she never used to do. On the contrary, she always admired him and envied his education. Now she tries to persuade him to write poetry again and to stop drinking, whereas the old Rita

accepted him as he was. Gradually their relationship becomes strained. She no longer attaches so much importance to their tutorials, at times coming late and
sometimes not turning up at all. She hardly shows any
interest in his private life and does not inform him about
changes in her own, such as her new flatmate, her
change of job or the fact that she now calls herself
Susan again. At one time he was the most important
person in her life, always the first to know about any
important new experience, such as the performance of
Macbeth. When he challenges her about this she turns
on him in anger, saying that such things are only
boring, minor details and that she prefers to discuss
more interesting subjects. Apparently she is referring to
the type of conversations she holds with students in the
bar where she works. She describes these new friends
as people who are 'not trapped' (Act 2, Scene 4). This is
reminiscent of Rita's former life, when she felt imprisoned by the limitations and prejudices of her
working class environment. She now seems to feel that
she has escaped to a world in which people are free of
such social pressures.

The tension between them eventually explodes in Act
2, Scene 5. Frank had asked for Rita's opinion on some
of his poems, which in itself is a reversal of their former
roles. He is bitterly disappointed when she gives him
sophisticated, second-hand opinions instead of her own
personal reactions. He has to recognise that his worst
fears have come true. The old Rita with her passionate,
honest responses to literature, has completely disappeared. Sarcastically, he suggests that a monster has
taken her place, a monster who is so blinded by her new
'culture' that she can no longer form judgements of her
own. He accuses her of being unable to tell what really
matters in life, unable to distinguish what is real from
imitation.

Then, suddenly, Rita's life takes a different turn again. Trish, the cultured woman she admires so much, has tried to kill herself. Shocked, Rita realises that her flatmate's sophisticated manners, her good taste and clever opinions on art and literature, were nothing but a shiny veneer, with no real substance behind it. She understands now that Frank is right. He had stood by and watched whilst she copied Trish and all the other called educated people around her. He had tried to warn her not to lose herself by copying others, but she had not listened. Once she had even accused him of deliberately trying to prevent her from reaching the same level as himself so that he could still look down on her. But she had been wrong. He really had been concerned about her. After taking her exam she goes back to thank him for everything and to admit that he had been right. She had indeed mistaken the appearance of culture for real education. Trish's attempted suicide makes it clear to her that there is more to life than art and literature.

By the end of the play Rita sees clearly what had happened to her. She had escaped from the confining attitudes of her original environment only to exchange one set of conventions for another. She had blindly taken over the accepted, orthodox opinions of so-called experts. Instead of an education, she had merely gained knowledge. But now, finally, she has acquired the freedom she was seeking without losing her personality. She has been trained to think in a more structured, analytical way and is able to make more informed choices. If she decides not to watch ballet or opera on TV it will be because she chooses not to and not from sheer prejudice.

Rita also has wider, more meaningful choices of what to do with her life. There are several immediate possibilities, for instance she could accompany Frank to Australia, go on holiday in France with a group of students or even spend Christmas with her parents. This last alternative shows that she has achieved a balance between her old self and the new. Knowing she now has the choice of whether to conform to the conventions of her old environment or not, she is able to contemplate the possibility of spending Christmas there. Russell himself makes the following comment about Rita's transformation:

At the end of the play what I'm trying to show is somebody who synthesizes the best of what she can gain from literature and what she can get from *Rubyfruit Jungle* ... One's talking about a complex woman. It's also, of course, something to do with class. I'm talking about somebody who synthesizes the best of two classes and trying to attack the divisions really in teaching, in education, and in the class system. And so it's the division and it's the elitist way in which literature is dealt with that I really object to. (Glaap,1984, p.22)

This balance between the old and the new, between Rita and Susan, the hairdresser and the student, is illustrated by her act of cutting Frank's hair in the last scene. She has come full circle, slipping back into the role of hairdresser, but with the all-important difference that she can now *choose* whether or not to work as a hairdresser.

FRANK

The first impression of Dr Frank Bryant, Rita's university tutor, does not inspire confidence. He obviously has a drinking problem. But we also learn from a phone conversation that he is witty, with a taste for irony and even sarcasm. Nevertheless, he represents a different culture and is Rita's key to a better way of life.

Frank did not aspire to being a university lecturer. In fact, he is really a poet. However, since he could not make a living from it he turned to lecturing in English literature. Over the years he has grown bored and frustrated and now, in his early fifties, he is disillusioned and cynical. Later, when Rita knows him better, she comments on his cynicism, suggesting that he hides his feelings behind this facade. And indeed, as the play progresses, we begin to understand that he is actually a very sensitive person, but has perhaps been so deeply hurt in the past that he now feels the need to protect himself.

Frank is frustrated with his work because he loves literature, but recognises that for the majority of his students a university degree is no more than a passport to a relatively affluent, secure future. And those who do show an interest in the subject soon learn which responses are expected. The essays which they hand in are full of conventional interpretations, supported by acceptable quotations from established literary authorities.

Frank's frustration extends to the whole of the literary establishment. He hates the smugness and pretentiousness of the so-called experts. At one point Frank explains to Rita that as a poet he made the mistake of trying to write 'literature', or the sort of work which would be acceptable to literary critics and could be studied and 'appreciated' by students. These days he no longer thinks he has anything important to say and has stopped writing poetry altogether. Today Frank feels that all he is really required to do is to relay traditional, conventional opinions on established authors to mediocre students so that they can pass exams. The only way he can face this task is with the help of alcohol. Drinking also helps him to forget or suppress his frustration in other areas of his life. He has split up from his wife and is now living with a former student called Julia, but his bitter remarks about both women suggest that he has also been very disappointed in his private life.

Then, suddenly, Frank is confronted with someone with a genuine love of literature and a burning desire to

learn. He immediately realises that this young hairdresser has a far greater thirst for learning than the average student. As their first meeting progresses he begins
to recognise that Rita is indeed quite unique. Although
her mind is completely untrained and she has absolutely no idea about literature, she is highly intelligent and
also very honest. Her total ignorance of literary studies
means that for the first time in his teaching career a student is not afraid to give him her spontaneous, emotional reactions to literature. This, together with her
originality and wit, makes him feel as if she is the first
breath of fresh air which has been in his room for years.
He is fascinated by her enthusiasm, unpredictability,
energy and her independent mind.

Yet Frank does not leap at the chance to teach Rita.
After she has explained her reasons for taking the
course he realises just how much it means to her. He
suspects that this will force him to examine his own
assumptions more closely and he is not sure whether
he really wants his rather boring, but comfortable existence to be disturbed to such an extent. He is probably
also afraid of being unable to fulfil Rita's demands.

Nevertheless, against his better judgement, Frank decides to accept his new student. It is as he feared. Her
complete ignorance about literature and traditional
methods of literary studies force him to explain and justify even the most basic concepts. He is often confused
and embarrassed when she asks him to explain things
which he had never really questioned, such as the
difference between light reading and 'good' literature.
Frank is aware that Rita with her untutored mind
is capable of responding to literature in a much
more direct, honest way than most of his students
and colleagues. Through Rita Russell is challenging
the esoteric attitudes of traditional university studies
by forcing Frank to question his own understanding

of his work and of himself. (For more details see Themes).

At various times throughout the play, Frank tries to explain why he does not really want to teach her. He is afraid that once she has learned the conventional methods of approaching literature she will suppress her refreshing spontaneity and honesty in order to pass exams. Worst of all, he himself would be responsible for any such change. But since she refuses to go to any other tutor he has to find a way of helping her to acquire the 'better culture' which she so desperately desires without destroying her uniqueness. Knowing how much her studies mean to her, it is impossible to refuse.

No matter how much Rita tells Frank about her background, he cannot really understand what she is up against. He does not seem to have had any contact at all with working class people. At most he may have a romanticised view of their way of life, based on what he has read in novels. Even after Rita has painted a depressing picture of working class culture he cannot see anything wrong with it as long as people believe they are happy. Unlike Rita, Frank does not think in political terms. Although he follows her argument about the link between poor education and limited choices, he does not really understand what this means to the people involved. Nor is he very interested. He is not as much aware of social class as Rita. Throughout the play she makes references to the differences between the classes. Indeed, her whole aim is to escape into a better educated social class.

Frank's insensitivity to Rita's position is also demonstrated when he invites her and her husband, Denny, to a dinner party at his house. It obviously does not occur to him that he is putting Rita in a very embarrassing position. Apart from the conflict it might cause between the couple, he does not consider how uncomfortable they would feel among his academic friends. When Rita does not turn up Frank reproaches her for upsetting the arrangements, but we suspect that really he was very disappointed. Rita is too ignorant of middle class academic culture to know that in his circles Frank, too, is an outsider. He despises this 'better culture' of which he is a part, the one Rita aspires to. He probably only found the thought of the dinner party bearable because of the prospect of Rita's company.

Rita has to spell out to him why she could not come. His lack of understanding once again shows that he is completely unaware of the difficulties facing people from her background. He is totally unsympathetic, first suggesting that she should see a psychiatrist, then asking why she does not simply give the course up if it is causing so many problems. He is unaware of all the sacrifices Rita has made and does not see that it is now impossible for her to revert to her former life. It is only when Denny throws her out that he finally begins to grasp just how much she has become alienated from her original environment.

Despite his continuing reservations, Frank perseveres in equipping Rita to pass exams. Eventually he has to admit that her work is no different from that of his other students. Rita is delighted and does not notice the irony in his remark. Sadly, Frank sees that his worst fears have been realised and that she now writes the standard type of essay which examiners expect. Her responses are no longer her own, but second-hand, no longer emotional and original, but controlled, analytical and full of references to accepted authorities.

As Rita becomes more proficient she grows away from Frank. He notices that she begins to develop other relationships and that he is not the most important person in her life any more. He is hurt that her classes mean so little to her that she sometimes arrives late or not at all. He also notices that she no longer informs him of changes in her private life, as she used to. When he tackles her about this she is offended, feeling that he is intruding. He is also hurt by her comment that she prefers to be with people who are 'not trapped'. Rita does not realise that he himself feels trapped. He is really a poet and does not fit into established academic life. It is partly this sense of failure which has made him turn to drink. But Rita does not understand this and, he feels, would no longer be interested. He sees that she is slipping away from him and becoming a stranger. Gradually, he begins to dislike the person she is changing into. At one point he even says he will be glad when she leaves. But Rita is blind to his despair at having lost the one person who had given his teaching some sense of purpose. He had looked forward to their tutorials and had even become dependent on them to brighten up his existence.

Frank's disappointment is acute when Rita returns from a summer school in London. He can cope with her changed appearance and attempts to influence him, trying to make him stop drinking and write poetry again. But he is devastated when she tells him she has already read the poems of William Blake. He had been saving them up to read with her. They mean a lot to him and he had been looking forward to seeing her reactions and to guiding her towards a better understanding of them. He is even more disappointed with the essay which she writes on Blake. Instead of expressing her own feelings she describes the poems in the sophisticated, but second-hand jargon of literary criticism. Frank feels betrayed. He was counting on what he thought was Rita's unspoiled mind to see Blake the way he does, emotionally and without over-complicating him.

Later, when Frank asks for Rita's opinion on his own poems, her reaction makes it clear to him that the person he knew and liked has completely disappeared, probably forever. As before, her views are not her own, but borrowed. Frank is in despair. He had asked for her thoughts in a last attempt to save their relationship, to bind her closer to him. Also, she is the only person he knows who will give him an honest opinion, or so he had thought. Angry and bitter, he tells her that he has created a monster. He has turned her into so much of an expert on literature that she now relies more on conventional, second-hand opinions than on her own. This is exactly what he was afraid would happen. He has been instrumental in making her suppress her originality and her emotions. He is so disappointed that he can no longer stand the sight of her.

Frank's request for Rita's opinions on his poems reverses their normal positions, for suddenly the student is supposed to judge the teacher. In fact, there are times when Frank very much resembles the old Rita, for instance in his request for a simple, emotional response to Blake's poems. Rita, on the other hand, prefers the kind of impersonal, objective analysis which he used to demand from her. Another aspect of this role reversal is Frank's new interest in Rita's private life. In the earlier stages of their relationship she was the one who asked the personal questions. These days, however, the only thing she wants to discuss with him is literature.

The growing tension between Frank and Rita comes to a head when he expresses contempt for her newly acquired culture. To him, knowing which books to read and having the 'right' furniture does not constitute being educated. On the contrary, he despises most of the so-called 'cultured' people around him. He particularly finds the way his cultured colleagues teach and expect him to teach literature soulless and limiting, as proved by Rita's development. For him education is more than the transmission of knowledge, skills and exam techniques. He tries to develop a person's whole being, appealing to the heart as well as the head.

At the beginning of the play Frank explained one of his teaching principles to Rita, that of allowing learners to find things out for themselves. He tries to achieve a balance between teaching the accepted code of literary studies and helping his students to become more sensitive and aware.

Besides allowing students to develop and discover things for themselves it is also a point in Frank's favour that, although he disliked what Rita was asking him to do, he respected her wishes.

After the quarrel in which Frank questioned the value of Rita's new-found culture they lose touch with each other for a while. They actually become so estranged that Frank does not even know that Rita has reverted to her old name of Susan. Having lost the one person who gave him some sense of purpose in life, he falls into an even deeper despair than before. Never again will he experience the same sense of purpose and fulfilment as he did with this eager young hairdresser. Under Rita's influence he had cut down on alcohol, but now there is no reason to control himself. One day he turns up drunk at a lecture, with the result that his superiors suggest a two year sabbatical in Australia.

As Frank is packing to leave the country, Rita comes in. She has taken her exam and wants to thank him for everything. She also admits that he had been right. She had been so enthusiastic about her new knowledge and skills that she had lost sight of herself. As she talks Frank recognises the old Rita re-emerging. They are now on the same level. There is not much more he can teach her about literature, so the dependence of the student on the teacher has disappeared. In fact, if anything it is Rita who is now the more dominant figure. Since they have found their way back to their old relationship Frank sees no reason why he should not invite her to accompany him to Australia. But Rita is just beginning to enjoy her independence and does not want to be pressed into making any decisions about her future yet. Typically, Frank does not insist, but allows her time to make up her own mind. The ending is left open. She might join him in Australia, but then again she might not. The last scene is a reminder of where Rita stood at the beginning of her studies. Once more she slips into her role of hairdresser as she prepares to 'take ten years off' him by cutting his hair. When asked about this ending Russell said that it was not intended to be anything more than a humorous gag. But literary students might defy him and interpret it as a symbol of the beginning of Frank's rejuvenation.

DENNY, RITA'S MOTHER, TRISH

Denny, Rita's mother and Trish are important because of their dramatic function in the play rather than for their individual characteristics.

Denny

Rita's husband Denny (short for Dennis) represents the inflexible attitudes and limited horizons which Rita finds so constraining. He has been brought up to believe that the man is the head of the household and that his wife should obey him. He cannot understand Rita's needs at all. She tries to explain and even attempts to involve him by inviting him to accompany her to the theatre. She also compromises by doing her studying at work in order to avoid arguments. But Denny stubbornly refuses to listen. Eventually he issues an ultimatum. She must either live with him on his terms, which means giving up her studies, or not at all.

Besides his function as a representative of the repressive culture from which Rita wants to escape, Denny's personality also forms a sharp contrast to Rita's. He is not a deep thinker and cannot understand what she means by a different quality of choice. He does not really see women as having much choice anyway. For him their only role in life is to become wives and mothers. Rita's rebellion completely baffles him. His world is one in which nothing ever changes. He is completely at home in an environment where choice is defined as eight different kinds of beer in the local pub. In this respect, too, he represents the kind of limited, inflexible mentality which Rita hates. At one point she explains to Frank that people from her background exert tremendous pressure on each other to conform. She feels that this is because they are afraid of change. Anyone who tries to break out is perceived as a threat and made to feel an outsider. Denny illustrates this kind of attitude by his refusal to try to understand his wife's needs. When it becomes clear that she will not revert to her former self, but is determined to alter her life, he rejects her. His refusal to contemplate any kind of change is stronger than the need to keep his wife. His attitude to change is expressed in his accusation that Rita has 'betrayed' him, meaning that by turning away from the traditional working class way of life she is also rejecting his norms and values.

Denny's reluctance to face up to problems is illustrated by the scene in the pub where Rita's mother starts to cry for no apparent reason. Instead of trying to find out what is wrong Denny cheers her up again. He probably realises what she is thinking, but refuses to allow anything to disturb the framework of traditional values on which he has built his life. At one point Rita explains to Frank that her husband is not so unintelligent that he would not be able to understand her, it is rather that 'he's blind, he doesn't want to see' (p.18, l. 31). The contrast with Denny's need for the security of traditional norms makes Rita's decision to break away seem all the more courageous.

Rita's mother

Rita's mother is important because she leads the kind of life her daughter would have if she accepted the traditional role of women. It is Mrs White's disappointment and frustration that makes Rita even more determined to avoid falling into the same trap herself.

Trish

Trish (short for Patricia) is only briefly mentioned, but it is obvious that Rita models herself on her flatmate, taking over her opinions and even, for a while, her way of speaking. Rita sees Trish as an embodiment of the 'better culture' which she herself is so desperately seeking. However, Trish's attempted suicide shows Rita that her flatmate's world is really very empty and that underneath the cultured exterior Trish's life is shallow and meaningless. Her suicide attempt makes Rita see that she herself had only exchanged one set of meaningless choices for another. She had been taken in by appearances such as the 'right' books on the shelves and by clever-sounding opinions. Trish's attempt to kill herself is the catalyst which makes Rita stop and think. From then on she is able to distinguish between real education and pretentiousness.

Themes

1. CULTURAL DIVISIONS BETWEEN THE SOCIAL CLASSES IN BRITAIN

Russell is very conscious of the differences between the social classes in Britain. Like Rita, he, too, was brought up in a working class family and left school early with very few qualifications. His reasons for taking up his education at a later stage were similar to Rita's, he 'wanted to know' what he had missed. He feels very strongly that education reinforces the division between the social classes and that the working class is at a great disadvantage. (For more details see Themes 2, 3).

Whilst being aware of differences in middle and working class cultures, Russell finds it difficult to define them. He actually denies that there is any such thing as a specifically 'working class culture', suggesting instead that it is a mixture:

> But is there a pure working-class culture? No, I don't think of it as pure because its a hybrid culture really ... I am aware of, without really being able to define it, the difference between a high art culture and what we, for the sake of convenience, call a working-class culture. And it's easier to define a high art culture than it is to describe the hybrid, working-class culture. (Jones 1989, pp.320-321)

There is, however, one point on which he is clear:

> I don't believe that you can give the working-class a middle-class culture, because a working-class culture is still based upon the word spoken and not the word written. It's still an oral-based culture and not a literary culture. A middle-class culture is a literary culture; information is carried in the written word. Still today in the working-classes the information and the code is dealt with in the spoken word and that's why it's terribly difficult to teach working-class kids, because teaching is a middle-class process: it's conducted by the middle-classes with reference to literature ninety-nine percent of the time. (Glaap 1984, pp.28-29)

Unlike some other playwrights and sociologists, Russell does not romanticise about the working class. Instead, he attacks the inflexibility which causes them to reject things which are not part of their traditions. He criticises the bigoted, conservative aspects of working class life which prevent individuals from developing. The theme of a working class person fighting to escape from a repressive family and community runs through his plays.

Attempts have been made to describe the cultural differences between the social classes. Longman's *Dictionary of English Language and Culture* (1992, p.1258) suggests the following categories:

– *Food*: The British middle classes are more likely to eat healthily and to try foreign food than the working class. This point comes out in Russell's play when Rita labels Frank as a 'Flora man' who eats 'pebble-dashed bread', meaning that he is health-conscious. Frank also mentions that his girl friend often prepares the French dish ratatouille. This would be very unusual in a working class home, where more traditional food would be served. It is also relatively rare for working class people to visit restaurants.

– *Education*: Given the choice, the middle classes would prefer to send their children to either public or grammar schools rather than comprehensives. They also encourage them to go on to college or university. Working class children almost always attend comprehensives and if they continue with their education after school-leaving age it will probably be at a college of technology or of education.

– *Work/jobs:* Whereas young middle class people often go into professions such as teaching, medicine or finance, their working class equivalents do less qualified work, for instance as hairdressers, mechanics, shop assistants or lorry drivers.

– *Housing*: Home ownership is higher among the middle classes. They tend to live in detached or semi-detached houses in the suburbs, as does Frank. The working class, on the other hand, often rent council houses or flats and often live in the inner cities, like Rita.

– *Leisure:* It is the middle class rather than the working class which enjoys the products of 'high culture', such as the theatre, museums and art galleries. Rita's suggestion that Frank watches BBC television rather than ITV is also substantiated by reality. Generally speaking, the middle class prefers the more serious programmes on BBC 2 and Channel 4 rather than the lighter entertainment on ITV.

Educating Rita illustrates another difference in leisure activities. Dinner parties, such as Frank's, are never given by the working class. They prefer to meet in pubs, like Rita's family, and working men's clubs. This explains Rita's ignorance about which wine to take to Frank's. Wine bars are usually preferred by the middle classes.

– *Sports and games*: Middle class sports tend to be cricket, golf, tennis, skiing and sailing, as opposed to the working class preferences for football, darts, horse racing, bingo, snooker and, in the north, racing pigeons.

– *Politics:* Traditionally the middle classes are associated with the Conservative and Liberal parties, whereas the working class have usually voted Labour, at least for the 'Old' Labour Party. These cultural differences are still highly important, especially in England. They have been described as 'the unseen skeletal structure of England' (*The Spectator*, 13 March 1993, p.10). Whenever two English people meet they immediately try to place each other in the social hierarchy. Giving the right signals makes the difference between being accepted as one of the in-group, 'us', or rejected as one of 'them'. Consider the following description of such cultural differences: 'the under-landscape of English life, the uninspected networks of admission and exclusion – that is the really significant thing (...) it relies on tiny little signals of acceptability and training of not-quite-rightness and not quite-usness' (*ibid.*, p.9; usness = 'us'-ness).

2. SOCIAL CLASS AND EDUCATION

The value of education for personal development is a thread which runs through Russell's work. Although *Educating Rita* does not have an overt political message, it certainly implies that education can be used as a tool for emancipating working class individuals. The immense popularity of the play indicates that audiences understand Rita's point of view. Some may even feel encouraged to follow her example. For Rita's progress illustrates that education is more than gaining access to a better job and a higher social class. It is also the means by which people can recognise and develop their own potential.

As Rita turns into an educated member of the middle class she leaves her working class environment behind. The question arises as to whether she was right to persevere with something which alienated her from her own kind. Russell himself answers this question: 'with English class structure the way it is Rita has to be better off for having taken her course of action' (*The Times Higher Educational Supplement*, 4 July 1980).

In an interview Russell once claimed that in Britain education is a social divider. His belief is still valid today. Rita is an example of one of the masses of young working class people who leave school with hardly any qualifications. In contrast, those whose parents can

afford public schools are almost automatically destined
to join the social elite. Unemployment is virtually
unknown, for instance, among former students of Eton
public school. In 1993 the headmaster estimated that
the figure was no higher than four percent and that,
even more significantly, it had not risen over the
previous five years. At that time sixteen of the top
hundred jobs in the City were held by old Etonians (*The
Spectator*, 13 March 1993, p.10).

3. EDUCATION, 'HIGH CULTURE' AND 'LOW CULTURE'

Whilst Russell's play propagates education as a
means of emancipation, at the same time it highlights
the dangers of passing on norms and values without
reflection. Education is presented as a potentially
liberating, but also limiting process if students' opinions are standardised. Through *Educating Rita* Russell,
who was once a teacher himself, examines the question
of the academic study of literature and expresses his
doubts about traditional teaching methods. Frank's
consistent attempts to dampen Rita's enthusiasm for
the literary theories which she picks up give voice to
Russell's fears that a spontaneous love of art can easily
be suppressed by traditional interpretation methods
and exam techniques. Frank does not want Rita to become so dependent on established literary criticism
that she is afraid of expressing her own ideas, especially
if they are unconventional.

Towards the end of the play Rita accuses Frank of
taking his own education for granted. Indeed, Russell
does seem to be suggesting that Frank lacks sympathy
and understanding for people in Rita's position. The
wider implication is that educated members of the
middle class, like Frank, know almost nothing about

the lives of those less privileged than themselves and, furthermore, do not care.

Through the figure of Frank, Russell expounds his belief that literary critics and traditional approaches to literature are partly responsible for the cultural division between the social classes. For Frank is part of what Russell calls the 'literature industry', composed of those who define, evaluate and teach literature:

> There's something I call the 'literature industry' which has sprung up and which I particularly loathe because it seems to me to put a huge barrier between the Ritas of this world who want to learn and literature itself. It probably comes out in my own sort of situation; for years and years and years I wouldn't pick a classical or known and regarded author from the book-shelves. I'd rather read a racy, accessible American novel or in-deed quality American novels because they were rarely classi-fied as literature ... (I'm) trying to attack the divisions really in teaching, in education, and in the class system. And so it's the division and it's the elitist way in which literature is dealt with that I really object to. (Glaap 1984, p.21)

Russell sees this 'literature industry' as part of a broader 'high art culture', which also incorporates other types of art. He attacks this industry for suggesting, firstly, that there is such a thing as 'high culture', secondly for deciding what belongs in this category and, lastly, for spreading the idea that these cultural pro-ducts are only intended for a very well educated mi-nority:

> High art is refined art – opera houses, poetry books, concert halls, theatres. Just as I don't want the class division, I really don't want those cultural divisions. I want the concert hall, and the opera stage, and the poetry book to mean just as much to Joe as they do to Joseph (...). How you ever achieve that, I don't know, but it would be better if you didn't have a high art culture and a polarized working-class culture (...). We do have a liter-ature industry, an opera industry, a theatre industry, and the spokesmen are generally people who think that art is only for the few (...). The shapers, the makers, of the stranglehold are the writers *about* it, the communicators about it, not the commu-nicators themselves. I know for example when first I wanted to write drama, I diligently read *Theatre Quarterly* and *Drama*

Magazine. I could feel all the time being pulled into one approved direction, one approved style. There was a Michael Radcliffe piece in *The Observer* that presents us with what he thinks we should go and see. And he wants us to be guilty about going to see what we do see. (Jones 1989, pp.321-322)

Russell argues that the working class has no access to that part of Britain's culture which is normally described as 'high' or 'highbrow'. This is partly due to their own attitudes. Rita explains to Frank that people from her class normally reject the 'higher' forms of art, such as ballet and opera, without even trying to understand them. They feel that such things are reserved for the better educated middle classes, whilst they themselves prefer the more easily accessible, 'lowbrow' products of the popular or mass-mediated culture. But besides criticising the attitudes of the working class themselves, Russell also blames the elitist way highbrow culture is presented to them. In an attempt to improve this situation he decided to write plays specifically for working class audiences:

Whilst the working-classes are accused of being philistines, there is a general attempt in this country to withhold culture from them (...). Literature is an invention by the middle-classes for their own benefit. The working-classes haven't accepted literacy yet, which is why it is so difficult teaching working-class kids whose traditions are in the spoken word. That's why I write for the theatre, because it's connected with the spoken rather than the written word. (Charles 1983, pp.20-21)

Russell's questioning of traditional definitions of 'high culture' is expressed particularly through the clash of Rita's and Frank's backgrounds in the first scene. To Rita best-sellers and classical authors are all literature of equal standing, all 'books'. When she asks Frank to explain the difference he is embarrassed, realising that he has never really thought about traditional notions of what exactly constitutes quality literature. The scene makes the audience aware that the definitions of some cultural products as 'highbrow' and others as 'light entertainment' are rather arbitrary. In fact, no such dividing line existed before about the middle of the nineteenth century. In 1834 some laws were passed which split drama theatres from music halls and other popular places of entertainment. The term *legitimate* was then used to refer to 'high culture' or drama, and *non-legitimate* for variety shows and cabaret. From this time on the working class were made to feel that the more popular types of entertainment were less valuable than other art forms. Since that time there has been a continuing discussion about which cultural forms are more important than others. The categories for defining them have also shifted over the years. This process is particularly well illustrated in the cinema. For instance, the early Chaplin films were once regarded as popular entertainment, but today they enjoy the status of classics.

Other Elements

SETTING

The whole play is set in Frank's office at the university where he teaches literature. The university itself is 'Victorian-built' and in the north of England. Whilst the geographical location reflects the author's preference for writing about people from his own part of the country, the type of building is associated with long-standing traditions. It underlines the theme of the traditional approach to literary studies at British universities. Frank's office is full of the books and papers which he needs for his work. Rita loves the room because it has 'taste'. It represents the 'better culture' she is seeking. Although she finds it a mess, she feels that it is somehow genuine, 'there's nothing phoney about it' (p.21). She tells Frank that this is the sort of room she wants to have one day. Her question, 'How do you make a room like this?' (p.21) could be interpreted as 'How do I become the cultured kind of person who would have this kind of room?'

Rita's reaction to Frank's room is very significant because as she begins to acquire her 'better culture' she moves into a flat with a young woman who also has the 'right' books on her shelves. But in contrast to Frank's room, that of her flatmate does not reflect a genuinely well-educated person, but one who has only acquired superficial knowledge and opinions. Whereas at the beginning of the play Rita instinctively recognises the true education and culture of Frank's environment, later she becomes blinded by pretentiousness and second-hand ideas. And indeed, Frank's shelves are well stocked with classical authors such as T.S.Eliot, Dickens and Chekhov. There is also a painting of a nude religious scene, which Rita immediately notices. The vocabulary she uses (p.9), also the fact that she mentions it at all, shows that she is a very direct, outspoken sort of person. The print is important, too, because of its 'good' quality. Rita is probably aware of the difference between the type of nude pictures which educated, cultured people have on their walls and the ones which she normally sees around her. By referring to the picture so openly she may also be testing Frank, as she does by swearing in front of him.

Frank's room not only illustrates the kind of work he does, but also the type of person he is, an intellectual with a thirst for reading and knowledge, and careless about conventional norms such as tidiness. The only non-intellectual note are the bottles of whisky hidden behind the books. They are an expression of his need to escape from his sense of futility and his lack of conviction about his social role. The coffee mug from which he drinks his whisky is a concession to his superiors. They know about his habit and are prepared to tolerate it as long as he keeps up appearances. There is a parallel between the university authorities and Denny, who also prefers to pretend that everything is fine instead of facing up to problems.

Another important feature of Frank's room is the window, which Rita says she loves. Through it she can see all the 'proper' students reading and studying on the lawn below. This view represents her idealised projections about educated people. Her wishful thinking forms a sharp contrast to Frank's disillusionment, 'I sometimes get an urge to throw something through it ... A student usually' (p.13). Frank hardly ever notices the view, but takes it for granted, just as he no longer notices the picture on the wall. This must seem like a mockery to Rita, who envies him his room so much. Because she is still in awe of universities and lecturers she does not recognise Frank's remark as his desire to escape from a world which he finds confining. Ironically, the same room represents freedom to the one person and imprisonment to the other.

The window takes on an additional symbolic meaning later in the play. In the first scene Frank describes Rita as 'the first breath of air that's been in this room for years' (p.18). However, when she tries to open it in Act 2, scene 1, it is stuck. It seems that with her refreshing originality gone, she is no longer able to let any air in. The window also has a symbolic meaning with regards to Frank. He is unhappy with the limitations imposed on him by traditional approaches to literature. A poet at heart, he inwardly rebels against teaching students the accepted ways of 'appreciating' literary works. But since he cannot live by writing poetry he has no other option. His sense of imprisonment is expressed in his physical environment.

Frank's room signifies both imprisonment and his retreat from the world. Not only is his window permanently closed, but it is also difficult to open the door from the outside. So other people cannot enter easily. Just as Rita feels imprisoned by her home environment, Frank is confined to a job he dislikes, symbolised by his confinement to one single room. The fact that Rita has difficulties opening Frank's door could also be read as a symbolic barrier preventing her from entering his world. Frank's only other social contacts, apart from Rita, are his students and Julia, his partner, but none of these relationships seem very satisfactory. Rita, on the other hand, is connected with several different locations, although we only hear about them – her home, the pub, the hairdressing salon and bistro where she works and summer school. Consequently, her social contacts are many and varied. Whereas Frank is only associated with one setting throughout the play, Rita's physical location changes as she moves from the home she shares with her husband to her mother's and then to a flat.

It is interesting that neither Frank nor Rita are able to enter the other's private sphere. Frank invites Rita to his home, but she feels unable to enter. Similarly, he would not be at home in her environment. This total separation between the physical locations could be interpreted as a symbol of the gulf which exists between the social classes. Both are completely ignorant of each other's home environment and interaction on a private level is impossible. It is only with great difficulty that Rita finally manages to penetrate into Frank's world.

Besides the window and door, another feature of Frank's room which takes on symbolic significance is his chair. During their first tutorials Frank always sits in a swivel chair. On one occasion he offers it to Rita, but she declines, saying, 'No. You're the teacher, you sit there' (p.21). It is interesting that Frank says it does not matter where he sits. He obviously does not need furniture to reinforce his authority. Later, however, after he turned up drunk to a lecture, he sits Rita down in his own chair and she no longer protests (p.66). This underlines her feeling that she is now on the same level as him and, in the present situation, even superior.

Significantly, when Rita and Frank reach the end of their time together, the room is emptied. It is as if the stage is being cleared for a new beginning. The packing up of the books marks the end of the teacher-student relationship. Everything is being removed so that something else can take its place. The clearing of the room signifies the end of something, but also a new beginning. Like the room, both Rita's and Frank's lives will be filled with new contents, as yet unknown. In Frank's case, the ambiguity of his future is reinforced by his destination. Australia is a country where prisoners used to be sent, but it is also a relatively new country.

As Frank himself says, 'Things are just beginning there' (p.77). Rita's future location is even more uncertain. She does not know where the next scene in her life will be set and, like Frank's room, does not know which people will be in it.

SYMBOLISM

Russell makes frequent use of symbolism to give additional meaning to a point he is making. The most obvious example is Rita's changes of name to underline her transformation from Susan, the uneducated hairdresser, to Rita, the admirer of an author of popular fiction, and then back again to Susan, as she rejects her own pretentiousness and accepts herself as she is. It is significant that the author whom Russell selects as the object of Rita's admiration, Rita Mae Brown, was one of the founders of both the women's and the gay movement. Rita's admiration for her prepares the audience to expect similar traits in Rita's personality.

All the works which Russell chooses for Rita's education have a symbolic significance. The one she starts with, E.M.Forster's *Howards End* is a parallel story to Rita's own: a young, working class man is living in poverty, but trying to educate himself. He knows that there is more to life than everyday existence and is searching for some deeper meaning to it. He loves literature and music, but the woman he lives with cannot understand him. By chance, he gets to know a wealthy, cultured family and at first tries to copy them. Eventually, however, he progresses beyond mere imitation. One element which is particularly relevant to Rita's story is a woman who acts as a link between different social classes. When her leisurely, cultured life is disrupted, she at first feels disoriented and isolated, but then manages to reconcile two apparently conflicting ways of life.

Russell's choice of *Howards End* is also significant

because of the now famous phrase with which Forster introduced it 'only connect'. As Rita's mind becomes better trained she is increasingly able to make new connections between various different phenomena. Frank proves to her, for instance, that her description of working class life is actually an illustration of the phrase (pp. 36-37).

When Rita suggests that the phrase describes how 'no-one does connect' in the novel (p.37) she is also unconsciously describing her own situation and that of Frank. At home Rita cannot connect in any meaningful way with those around her and the same can be said of Frank. As the play develops, the relationship between Rita and Frank deteriorates and they, too, find that they can no longer connect with each other. The phrase is also a comment on Rita as she is at the end of the play, when she seems able to combine her past with her present. After a period of alienation from her original background, she can contemplate spending Christmas at her parents'.

Having finally come to terms with *Howards End*, Rita moves on to Ibsen's play *Peer Gynt*. Again, this choice underlines Rita's own situation. She herself refers to it as the story of someone 'searchin' for the meanin' of life' (p.35). At the end of the nineteenth century Ibsen shocked audiences with his realism and by writing about topics such as a woman's right to leave her husband and create her own life.

After Ibsen, she progresses to Chekhov, a dramatist whose characters cannot relate to each other and who hide the frustation and emptiness of their lives behind a facade. This choice of author is an indirect comment on the lives of most of the characters in *Educating Rita* – Rita herself, Frank, Mrs White and Trish. Rita's increasing familiarity with Chekhov underlines the break-up of her relationship with Frank.

During the summer school course Rita not only learns about Chekhov, but also about the poet William Blake. Once more, Russell is making an indirect comment on her progress. Blake wrote two sets of poems, the *Songs of Innocence* and the *Songs of Experience*. The first set, the *Songs of Innocence*, describes ideals and childlike innocence; the second is often bitter in tone and shows how these ideals turn into illusions in the face of reality. Tellingly, the poem which Rita learns off by heart, *The Sick Rose*, is one of the *Songs of Experience*. This choice of poems gives additional significance to Rita's progression from a state of innocence regarding the study of literature to one of experience. But the selection of a poem from the second collection could be a hint that her dreams might not be fulfilled, or at least not in the way she expects.

Another interesting literary reference is to a novel by Somerset Maugham, *Of Human Bondage*. Although only briefly mentioned, it touches on one of the main ideas of the play, that of imprisonment. Both Rita and Frank feels imprisoned by their environment and, eventually, both manage to escape. In Frank's case Russell's choice of Australia as his new destination might be a hint that he is really only exchanging one 'prison' for another. There are many feature of Frank's office which symbolically reinforce this theme. (See Setting)

Besides Rita's changes of name, the most overt symbol of her progress is in the last scene, when Frank 'rewards' her with a present of a dress 'for an educated woman friend' (p.77). This is a reminder that when Rita started her course she vowed not to buy a new dress until she had passed her first exam and then it would be 'a proper dress, the sort of dress you'd only see on an educated woman' (p.24). Frank's present acknowledges her successful transformation into just such a person.

Form and Structure

The play consists of a series of conversations between Rita and her tutor, Frank, all set in Frank's university office. It traces the process by which the two get to know each other and at the same time discover themselves. Because attention is focussed on psychological processes rather than events the pace is rather slow. Given the limited number of characters and settings it is interesting how Russell still manages to sustain the audience's interest. The first meeting between the two characters is very lively and amusing, partly because of Rita's outspokenness and sense of humour, and partly because of some comical misunderstandings arising from discrepancies in their knowledge of literature.

As the first Act progresses the tone becomes more serious. Rita realises how much she has to learn and Frank becomes increasingly aware of the huge responsibility he has taken on. Variety is provided by the introduction of Rita's husband, Denny. Although he never actually appears, his presence is felt very strongly because of the restrictions he imposes on his wife's studies. Denny is an underlying source of tension, keeping the audience wondering if Rita will manage to continue with her education in the face of his growing opposition. The conflict between husband and wife gradually escalates up to the point where Denny burns Rita's books (scene 5). However, the mood quickly reverts to one of calm when Rita insists on discussing her work instead of her marriage.

Throughout the play Frank and Rita's conversations about literature are interspersed with information about their private lives. This provides a variety of different topics, thus sustaining the audience's interest. One example of this alternation between academic subjects and personal details is Act 1, scene 6, which begins rather startlingly when Rita bursts unexpectedly into Frank's office. The explanation is that she was so overwhelmed by a production of *Macbeth* the night before that she had to come and tell him about it.

Typically, the conversation switches from the personal to the academic as Frank takes the opportunity to explain the dramatic meaning of the term 'tragic'.

Towards the end of the first Act Rita's education takes a more serious turn when she suddenly realises that she is now in a no-man's-land, belonging neither to her original culture, nor to Frank's academic world. Rita, like the play itself, has arrived at a half-way mark and we wonder yet again whether she will be able to fulfil her dream of finding a 'better culture'. The crisis deepens because of Frank's lack of understanding. A calmer mood is introduced with Rita's decision, at the end of scene 7, to carry on with her education. But just as the audience settles back, imagining that things will run a little more smoothly from now on, another crisis arises. This time it is Denny who has provoked it by throwing his wife out. As before, Rita refuses to discuss the problem and the conversation reverts to her studies.

By the end of the first Act the play and Rita have reached a half-way stage. For her there is no alternative but to go on with her studies. She has become alienated from her original, working class environment and her marriage is over. The end of the first Act also represents a half-way point for Frank, because this is his last chance to decide whether to accept the responsibility of teaching Rita, with all that it entails, or not. His periodic doubts about teaching her during Act 1 give the play an additional source of tension.

Educating Rita is a very symmetrical work. It is

divided roughly into two halves, the first dealing more with Rita and the second with Frank. This symmetry is underlined by parallels in the development of both characters. Both feel alienated from and imprisoned by their original environments and in both cases their relationships with their partners break down. Rita's two crises towards the end of Act 1 are paralleled in Act 2 by Frank's increasing despair, which culminates in an enforced sabbatical.

After Rita's crises in Act 1 the second half of the play starts off in a more settled way. A course at summer school has firmly established Rita's identity as a student and Frank has apparently decided to continue teaching her. Interest now shifts to Frank. From the beginning of Act 2 he displays increasing signs of dissatisfaction with the 'new' Rita. Tension between them mounts and eventually explodes in a clash over Rita's interpretation of a poem by William Blake in scene 3.

During the second Act the two characters grow further apart as they develop in opposite directions. The introduction of Rita's flatmate, Trish, revives interest and introduces a new theme. For Rita is so impressed by Trish's cultured life-style that she adopts her as a model. Later, Trish's suicide attempt is the catalyst which eventually leads to the restoration of good feelings between Rita and Frank.

As Rita gradually establishes her position in the academic world, Frank becomes increasingly unacceptable there. The disappearance of the 'old' Rita makes him all the more conscious of the limitations and dangers of his university work. His deepening sense of despair and frustration and his growing need for alcohol finally lead to his professional downfall. Like Rita at the end of Act 1, Frank is now in a state of crisis.

During this time Frank and Rita seem to exchange

roles. Whereas Frank was the dominant partner in Act 1, in the second Act it is Rita who gradually assumes this role. By the end of the play she feels thoroughly at home in Frank's world, whereas he has been expelled from it. Again there is a parallel to Rita's life, for at the end of Act 1 she, too, had been expelled from her original environment.

The tension between the two comes to a head in scene 5 of Act 2, when Frank describes Rita as a monster. For a while there is almost no contact between them. In the following scene Russell uses the device of a telephone call to keep the action going, although there is only one person on stage.

The play ends on a harmonious, though ambiguous note. Rita and Frank have re-established their former relationship, but will go their separate ways, at least in the near future. This last scene emphasises the similarities between them. Both are at a crossroads. For both one phase of their lives is over and they must start on something new. Act 1 showed how they accompanied each other for a while, Act 2 described how they started to go different ways and now, at the end of the play, they have come together again. Besides the changing relationship between the two characters, the various stages of their separate developments provide a constant source of interest.

Style

The most striking feature of Russell's style is his use of a strong Liverpool dialect and his sense of humour. Indeed one critic even speaks of his 'sparkling Liverpool humour that has since become his trademark' (Charles 1983, p.21). Apart from a brief phase when Rita tries to imitate her flatmate's upper class way of speaking, she retains her Liverpool accent throughout the play. She does, however, drop the more vulgar expressions as she joins the ranks of the educated middle classes.

During the course of the play Rita's speech is affected by her studies. Having to analyse literature forces her to describe her reactions to it in more differentiated way. At the beginning of her studies she finds it very difficult to put her thoughts into words and often has to fall back on 'fillers' such as 'y' know' and 'like'. Later, however, as her thinking becomes more differentiated, she expresses herself more precisely and more fluently.

Rita's early use of language is typical of the so-called 'restricted code' of the working class, especially the lower working class. Characteristic features of this 'restricted code' are: a limited range of vocabulary, simple sentence structures, sentences often unfinished and the repeated use of fillers (y' know).

Rita's speech forms a sharp contrast with Frank's more formal use of language. He is able to put his thoughts together fluently in longer, more complicated sentences and does not need so many 'fillers'. His vocabulary is wider and more sophisticated and in comparison to Rita' sloppy pronunciation, his is more precise.

Rita is very conscious of the social prestige attached to the way educated people like Frank speak English.

Since the beginning of the twentieth century the standardised accent which Frank uses, generally known as
RP or Received Pronunciation, has been associated
with a high social standing and a good education. Although RP is only spoken by about 3% of the popu-
lation, its influence is enormous. Many people who
have been brought up with regional dialects prefer to
modify them in order to improve their chances of
moving up in society or to make themselves more
acceptable to their environment. Although the situation
is less extreme than it used to be, dialect speakers
can still find themselves at a disadvantage. Apparently,
the most unacceptable accents are those of Liverpool ('Scouse'), Birmingham ('Brummie') and Glas-
gow:

> The long-held suspicions of Scousers, Brummies and others
> that they suffer discrimination at work or when applying for
> jobs because of their accents has been borne out by new re-
> search.The accents of Liverpool, Glasgow and Birmingham are
> regarded by some employers as particularly 'negative', a survey
> of recruitment consultants has found (...) Former Arsenal and
> England footballer Alan Smith now writes on soccer for *The
> Daily Telegraph*, but fears his Birmingham accent would ob-
> struct a move into broadcasting (...) Edwina Currie, Tory MP for
> Derbyshire South and originally from Liverpool, admitted to
> adapting her accent to the nature of her audience. She said,
> 'I used to have a really strong Scouse accent (...), but it has soft-
> ened a bit now.' (*The Weekly Telegraph*, 8.-14. Jan. 1997, p.6)

Pygmalion and *Educating Rita* – A comparison

Educating Rita has often been described as a modern version of G. B. Shaw's play *Pygmalion* and there are certainly some striking similarities. Indeed, Shaw's innovative 'drama of ideas' paved the way for plays like *Educating Rita*, which are more concerned with psychological processes than external action. Both dramas deal with the changing relationship of a female student and her male teacher and both are set almost exclusively in the teacher's study.

Although *Educating Rita* was written about seventy years after *Pygmalion*, both focus on the same problem, namely the injustice of the English class system and the poor quality of the education offered to the working class. Both plays suggest that society would be more democratic if the barriers between the social classes were broken down and both see education as a key factor in this process. The serious messages in the two dramas are made more palatable by a sense of humour which is sometimes direct and sometimes more sophisticated and cynical.

Each play begins with a young working class woman trying to improve the quality of her life. But this is where the similarity ends. Shaw's heroine, Eliza Doolittle, is a flower girl in London's Covent Garden Market. When she is given the chance to learn to speak like a lady she seizes it because she sees the opportunity to improve her standard of living. Russell's heroine Rita, a Liverpool hairdresser, has more spiritual needs. She is frustrated by the lack of mental stimulation in her environment and wants to escape to a world with a 'better culture'. In trying to lead a more meaningful life Rita rejects the traditional role of women, which causes conflict with her husband. Her attempt to break out of a confining environment is regarded by those around her as a betrayal of their own way of life. Through Rita's struggle Russell is attacking the inflexible attitudes which often characterise the British working class. He feels that the pressures to conform can prevent working class individuals from developing. In this the two authors are very similar, for Shaw also hated conformity and inflexibility. Both Rita and Eliza are warnings that potential can go unrecognised in a rigid class system.

Pygmalion demonstrates that in Britain one of the barriers between the social classes and a major cause of injustice is the prestige attached to Standard British English and RP. The fact that a girl from the slums learns to speak like a lady proves that this barrier can be broken down by anyone with the necessary talent and energy. The social barriers which Russell wants to destroy are those erected by the way a nation's culture is transmitted. He blames the categories of 'high' and 'low culture' for reinforcing the divisions between the classes and particularly attacks traditional methods of teaching literature. Besides criticising elitist attitudes to culture he would like the education system to make more of an effort to appeal to the working class. Both *Pygmalion* and *Educating Rita* turn on the idea that people are capable of fulfilling their potential if they are only given the opportunity, regardless of their origins. Without this opportunity, the Lizas and Ritas of this world will remain deprived.

Both Rita and Eliza are exceptional individuals, alert, intelligent, quick to learn and with lively, original minds. At the beginning of their education both speak a very strong dialect. Besides adding a sense of realism, the dialect and colourful local expressions enliven the dialogue and often produce comical effects. Russell's play has a more authentic tone than Shaw's because the speech always sounds realistic. Shaw, on the other hand, often uses his characters as mouthpieces for his own ideas, which sometimes makes them sound stilted and unnatural.

As Eliza learns to be a lady her local dialect is completely eradicated, whereas Rita's is only modified. This is a reflection of changes in attitudes to regional dialects since Shaw's time. In the process of acquiring their education both women's speech becomes more controlled and standardised, losing some of its liveliness and originality. The implication is that although education is a liberating process, there may be a price to pay. Russell in particular stresses the danger that traditional teaching methods can suppress the students' spontaneity.

A further price of the two women's education is their alienation from their working class backgrounds. Rita realises that she has become something of an outcast approximately half-way through the play, when she finds herself unable to accept her tutor's invitation to a dinner party at his house. Eliza, too, reaches a point when she no longer belongs to her original environment, but is not yet part of any other culture. Eliza's sense of alienation turns to despair because, unlike Rita, she is no longer able to earn a living. When she first asked Higgins for lessons she was not aware of the possible consequences of her education. All she had seen was the chance of getting a job in a flower shop instead of selling her wares on the streets. Unlike Rita, she had felt at home in her environment and had not wanted to change in a more basic way. Rita, on the other hand, had dreamed of becoming a completely different person, one who could appreciate 'culture'. Consequently, when Rita passes her first exam she is happy and fulfilled, whereas Eliza is perhaps not entirely convinced of the value of her efforts.

The alienation of both women from their former cultures makes the point that education is not only the acquisition of certain knowledge and skills, but also involves learning a whole new set of social conventions, a new code, and that this affects the whole personality. When Eliza fails her first test at Mrs Higgins's it becomes obvious that in order to be accepted in polite society it is not enough to improve her pronunciation, vocabulary and grammar. Like Rita, she needs no less than a complete education. These changes of personality are underlined in both cases by outward signs such as a different style of dressing and a change of name.

Neither Higgins nor Frank can understand their students' distress at suddenly finding themselves in a cultural no-man's-land. Their lack of understanding and compassion are a criticism of the better educated members of society for ignoring the situation of the less privileged. But unlike Higgins, Frank appreciates Rita's personality. In fact, he admires her originality so much that he has grave misgivings about changing her. Whereas Higgins tries his best to transform Eliza, Frank desperately wants Rita to stay herself. Frank's sensitivity and sense of responsibility towards his student form a stark contrast to Higgins. It is because Frank is so intensely aware of the consequences of Rita's education that he becomes more and more frustrated and despondent as her studies progress.

Frank's doubts about his teaching are intensified through his contact with Rita. They are an expression of Russell's questioning of academic approaches to literature and 'high culture' altogether. Higgins, on the other hand, has no such doubts and it is for this that Shaw criticises him. He is so passionate about his work and the experiment that he completely ignores Eliza's feelings and does not once consider the possible consequences for her. He regards Eliza as his creation – a fact which is underlined by the reference to the legend of *Pygmalion* – and is proud of his success. In contrast, Frank hates the transformation he has effected in Rita and even suggests that he has created a monster.

Both plays reach a climax with a quarrel between teacher and student. Eliza realises that Higgins is not interested in her as a person, but only as an object for his experiments. Suddenly she sees how he has exploited her for his own prestige. Frank and Rita quarrel for a completely different reason. Frank is so frustrated and disappointed with the results of his efforts that he can no longer stand the sight of Rita. All his doubts about the value of his work are illustrated by the changes in her. Higgins, on the other hand, only thinks about the consequences of his work when Eliza forces him to. But the last scene clearly shows that he neither understands Eliza, nor does he gain any insights into his own behaviour.

As both women become more proficient they approach the same level of knowledge as their teachers. They also become much more self-confident. In fact, whereas the teachers started off being the more dominant partners, at the end it is the women who seem to be in control. Frank gradually becomes dependent on Rita to give him a sense of purpose in his work and Higgins relies on Eliza to organise the practical details of his life. But whereas Frank is able to adapt to Rita's new personality, Higgins remains totally inflexible. The final scene illustrates that he is unable to see Eliza as anything other than his creation, a creature inferior to himself whom he can continue to bully and order about.

Frank, on the other hand, can accept his former student as his equal, so much so that he invites her to accompany him to Australia. He has the gratification of recognising that, after all, his work has been worthwhile and that he has not destroyed the very qualities he admired in Rita.

At the end both women have gained in practical and spiritual terms. Besides adding to their knowledge and skills they have developed a stronger sense of their own value as people. The endings are left open. The two former students are now strong enough to make their own way in life without the help of their teachers. Just as Eliza refuses to return home with Higgins, Rita decides not to accompany Frank to Australia, at least not in the near future.

Through education both women have moved up into a higher social class. More importantly, they have been able to develop their own potential. However, whilst Rita has become completely integrated in the middle class, we learn from Shaw's Afterword that Eliza remains something of a social misfit. This is a typical expression of the author's refusal to romanticise about the possibilities of climbing the social ladder. Eliza certainly proves that a working class person can benefit from education, but even with Pickering's help it is impossible for her to become an accepted member of the upper class.

Both Shaw and Russell see education as the key to women's emancipation, but because of changes in the social role of women and in the class system Rita has more practical alternatives than Eliza. The former flower girl has improved her standard of living and social prestige. Rita's progress, on the other hand, is defined in terms of personal freedom and human dignity. In the last scene she returns to thank Frank, 'Because of what you'd given me I had a choice'.

Bibliography

Text Editions

Russell, Willy: *Educating Rita.* Samuel French, London 1981.

Russell, Willy: *Educating Rita.* Diesterweg, Frankfurt/Main 1997.

Russell, Willy: *Educating Rita.* Longman Literature 1991.

Selected Bibliography

Allan, P./Benyon, J./McCormick, B. (eds.): *Focus on Britain 1994.* Perennial Publications, Oxford 1994.

Chambers, C./Prior, M.: *Playwrights' Progress.* Amber Lane Press Ltd., Oxford 1987. An analysis of post-war British drama. Russell is one of a group of playwrights whose aim is to broaden the class basis of the theatre. They concentrate on regional rather than mainstream theatre and write about class for working class audiences.

Charles, Timothy: 'The First Ten Years'. In: Drama. 2nd Quarter 1983, No.148, pp.20-21. Published by The British Theatre Association. 9 Fitzroy Sq., London W1P 6AE.

Debusscher, Gilbert: *Educating Rita or an Open University Pygmalion.* In: Communicating and Translating. Essays in Honour of Jean Dierickx. Debusscher/van Noppen, Brussels University 1985, pp.303-317.

Dictionary of English Language and Culture, Longman, Harlow 1992.

Gill, John: *Willy Russell and His Plays.* Countyvise Ltd., Birkenhead 1996. An extensive interview with Russell covering his dramas, his social background and his political intentions. Also includes descriptions of all his plays and a comprehensive bibliography.

Glaap, A.-R.: *Willy Russell: Educating Rita. Comments and Study Aids.* Diesterweg, Frankfurt/Main 1984. A short collection of comments and study aids on *Educating Rita* and a lengthy interview with Russell himself.

Jones, Christopher N.: *Populism, the Mainstream Theatre, and the Plays of Willy Russell.* UMI Dissertation Information Services. Ann Arbor, Michigan 1989. An analysis of the relationship between popular theatre and contemporary mainstream British theatre, with Russell as a representative of the former. Includes an extensive interview with Russell.

The Spectator: 'We are doing very well, thank you', 13 March 1993, p.10.

The Times Higher Educational Supplement: 'What Rita lost along with the shampoo and sets', 4 July 1980.

Townroe, C./Yates, G.: *Sociology.* Longman, Harlow 1995.

The Weekly Telegraph: 'How you say things puts the accent on success', 8.-14. Jan. 1997, p.6.

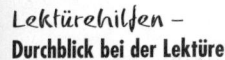